Contents

The College of West Anglia
Learning Resource Centre

Introduction

This pack has been developed for tutors teaching the CACHE award or certificate in Caring for a Child/Children at Entry Level 3 or the award, certificate or diploma in Caring for Children at Level 1. We hope that this Teaching Resource Pack will help you to consolidate and extend the learning topics in the core syllabus and prepare learners for their assessments.

What does the Teaching Resource Pack contain?

These teaching resources contain an exciting range of teaching ideas and activities so that you can select those that are most suitable for your learners. All the materials in the printed file can be photocopied and are also included on the @t work CD-ROM in Microsoft® Word format so that you can edit them before printing.

Printed materials

The printed materials are organised in chapters, matching the sequence of the chapters in the Heinemann *CACHE Entry Level 3/Level 1 Caring for Children Student Book*. Each chapter contains:

- Introduction and tutor notes
- Overview of resources
- Activity Sheets and Handouts

Chapter Introduction

This lists the learning outcomes of all the units covered in the chapter and contains information for delivery of the topic, together with suggestions for further sources of information – both print and online – to which you might like to direct learners. Solutions to questions on the activity sheets are also given here. (Please note that solutions are only given where there are clear 'right' or 'wrong' answers; where learners' own answers can be accepted, this is left to the tutor's discretion.)

Overview of Resources

This shows how the materials in the pack relate to the learning outcomes and assessment criteria. They also show where resources in the pack link to content in the Heinemann *CACHE Entry Level 3/Level 1 Caring for Children Student Book*, enabling you to use the pack effectively alongside the textbook.

Activity Sheets and Handouts

These consolidate and extend learners' knowledge and understanding. All activity sheets and handouts carry a direct reference to an assessment criterion, making it easy to help learners prepare for assessment. Care has been taken to make the activities relevant to the learners, and to prepare them for situations that they may encounter if they progress to work with children.

CACHE
Foundation Learning
Entry 3 / Level 1

Jacqueline Gut

Hayley Marshall

Ann Tapp

CARING FOR

CHIL

Teaching R

The College of West Anglia
Learning Resource Centre

Heinemann is an imprint of Pearson Education Limited, Edinburgh Gate, Harlow, Essex, CM20 2JE.

www.pearsonschoolsandfecolleges.co.uk

Heinemann is a registered trademark of Pearson Education Limited

Text © Pearson Education Limited 2011

The rights of Jacqueline Gut, Hayley Marshall and Ann Tapp to be identified as authors of this work have been asserted by them in accordance with the Copyright, Designs and Patents Act 1988.

First published 2011

14 13 12 11 10
10 9 8 7 6 5 4 3 2 1

British Library Cataloguing in Publication Data
A catalogue record for this book is available from the British Library

ISBN 978 0 435 04753 5

Produced by Tag Publishing Services
Original illustrations © Pearson 2011
Illustrated by Tag Publishing Services and Angie Stevens
Cover design by Sam Charrington
Cover photo © Getty Images: Reggie Casagrande
Picture research by Harriet Merry
Printed in the UK by Ashford Colour Press

Acknowledgements
The author and publisher would like to thank the following individuals and organisations for permission to reproduce logos and photographs:
p64: Lion Mark reproduced with permission of the British Toy & Hobby Association

Presentations: Ch1, S3, Bananastock/Imagestate, S5, Libby Welsh/Janine Wiedel Photolibrary/Alamy; Ch2, S2, Fancy/Alamy, S6, Lord and Leverett/Pearson Education Ltd; Ch3, S3, ifong/Shutterstock, S4, Wavebreakmedia Ltd/Shutterstock; Ch4, S2, Gareth Boden/Pearson Education Ltd, S5, Jovan Nikolic/Shutterstock, S7, S.Wanke/Photolink/Photodisk; Ch5, S3, Jules Selmes/Pearson Education Ltd, S5, Lisa Payne Photography/Pearson Education Ltd; Ch6, S3, Jules Selmes/Pearson Education Ltd; Ch7, S3, MN Studio/Shutterstock, S5, Jules Selmes/Pearson Education Ltd; Ch8(1), S4, Food Photography Eisig/Corbis; Ch8(2), S2, Jules Selmes/Pearson Education Ltd, S4, Studio 8/Pearson Education Ltd; Ch9(1), S2, Sarah2/Shutterstock, S3. Lusoimages/Shutterstock; Ch9(2), S4, Jesse Reardon/Twila Reardon/Corbis; Ch10(1), S5, Studio 8/Pearson Education Ltd; Ch10(2), S5, Karen Roach/Shutterstock
Knowledge checks: Ch2: Pearson Education Ltd/ Jules Selmes; Ch4: Shutterstock/ Hysteria; Ch6: a. Pearson Education Ltd/Tudor Photography, b. Pearson Education Ltd/ Jules Selmes, c. Shutterstock/ HomeStudio, d. Shutterstock/Lori Sparkia, e. Shutterstock/motorolka; Ch7: Pearson Education Ltd/Tudor Photography

Every effort has been made to contact copyright holders of material reproduced in this book and CD-ROM. We apologise in advance for any unintentional omissions. Any omissions will be rectified in subsequent printings if notice is given to the publishers.

CD-ROM resources

In addition to Word files of all the printed resources, the following additional resources are contained on the CD-ROM inside this pack:

- Interactive Knowledge checks
- PowerPoint presentations.

The resources are organised by chapter and accessed from a central menu.

Interactive knowledge checks

The Knowledge checks or 'quizzes' cover the key learning points within a chapter and will engage learners directly. They can be used to gauge learners' levels of knowledge before you begin teaching a topic and again after you have finished the topic so that you and the learners can see how they've progressed in their understanding. The quizzes are suitable either for whole-class or group work, or for more able learners to access independently via the VLE.

Please note: Your browser security may initially try to block elements of this product. If this problem occurs, please refer to the Troubleshooting document, which can be found in the root of the CD-ROM.

PowerPoint® presentations

The ready-made presentations will save you time and use colourful images and graphics to draw attention to key topics and stimulate class discussion.

How to use the @t work CD-ROMs ⊙ work

This Teaching Resource Pack includes two @t work CD-ROMs full of high-quality, visual interactive resources designed to help you motivate your learners.

1. The **CACHE Entry Level 3/Level 1 Caring for Children Teaching Resource Pack @t work CD-ROM**, which can be used in conjunction with an interactive whiteboard, contains:

   - Word files of all the materials you have in the printed file so you can adapt and customise them to suit your own teaching
   - Interactive resources to use with your learners.

This product can be run straight from the CD-ROM, or installed to your local hard drive or to the network. When this disk is loaded into a CD/DVD drive on a PC it should autorun automatically. If it does not, please browse the disk and double-click RB32.bat. Further instructions on how to do this are available from the central menu.

2. The **CACHE Entry Level 3/Level 1 Caring for Children Teaching Resource Pack @t work CD-ROM VLE version** contains exactly the same resources as the CACHE Entry Level 3/Level 1 Caring for Children Teaching Resource Pack @t work CD-ROM, but formatted so that they can easily be uploaded to your VLE. Please follow the usual instructions specific to your VLE system to upload this SCORM 1.2 Content Pack.

Please note: Both of the **CACHE Entry Level 3/Level 1 Caring for Children Teaching Resource Pack @t work CD-ROMs** are suitable for use on a Windows® PC only. They will not run on Macintosh OS X.

System requirements for the **CACHE Entry Level 3/Level 1 Caring for Children Teaching Resource Pack @t work CD-ROMs:**

OS: Windows XP* sp2. RAM: 512MB (1GB for Vista) 1GHz processor (2GHz for Vista)

Microsoft Office 2003*, Adobe Flash Player 9*, Adobe Reader 8*, Internet Explorer 7*/Firefox 3

*or later versions

CACHE Entry Level 3/Level 1 Caring for Children units covered

The following units are covered in the Heinemann **Entry Level 3/Level 1 Caring for Children Student Book** and **Teaching Resource Pack**.

Unit number	Unit title	Level	Credits
CFC1	Confidence building for the young child through play	E3	3
CFC2	Listening to and talking with a young child	E3	3
CFC3	Providing a safe and hygienic environment for a young child	E3	3
CFC4	Routines for a young child	E3	4
CFC5	Play and learning in the home	E3	3
CFC6	Responsibilities of new parent(s)	E3	3
CFC7	Eating healthily	E3	3
CFC8	Contraception information	E3	1
IRRE3	Individual rights and responsibilities	E3	1
CFC9	Respecting and valuing children	1	2
CFC13	Sharing learning experiences with children	1	4
CFC14	Growth and development of young children	1	2
CFC15	Human growth and development	1	2
CFC16	Preparing for your next steps	1	4
CFC17	Supporting babies to play	1	3
CFC19	Self development	2	3
CFC20	Healthy eating for families	1	4
CFC21	Science activities for young children	1	3
CFC23	Musical activities for young children	1	2
CFC24	Practical health and safety when with young children	1	3
–	Understand play for early learning	1	3
HL1	Healthy living	1	2

Qualification coverage
in the Heinemann CACHE Entry Level 3/Level 1 Student Book

Level/Unit	Learning outcomes and Assessment criteria	Chapter	Student Book page number
E3 IRRE3 Individual rights and responsibilities	**1. Understand that they have individual rights and responsibilities.**	1	2–7
	1.1 Describe an individual right which is relevant to them.		2–3
	1.2 Identify sources of support or information about rights and responsibilities.		2–3
	1.3 Describe a responsibility that they have for themselves.		4
	1.4 Describe a responsibility that they have to others.		5
L1 CFC14 Growth and development of young children	**1. Know about factors which influence growth and development of children from birth to 5 years 11 months.**	2	10–21, 26–27
	1.1 Outline the patterns and stages of growth for children from birth to 5 years 11 months.		10–17
	1.2 Identify factors which influence growth and development from birth to 5 years 11 months.		18–19
	1.3 State the importance of diet and exercise for children's growth and development		20–21
	2. Know how to support growth and development of children.		22–27
	2.1 Identify activities which promote children's physical development		22–23
	2.2 Outline ways to help children to develop communication and language skills		24–25
	2.3 Describe ways to encourage children to play socially		25
L1 CFC15 Human growth and development	**1. Know about human growth and development.**	2	28–36, 40–41
	1.1 Identify the main stages of growth and development across the human lifespan.		28–33
	1.2 Outline what is meant by physical, intellectual, emotional and social development		34–35
	2. Know factors which affect human growth and development.		36–41
	2.1 Identify factors which may affect physical growth and development		36–37
	2.2 Outline circumstances or life events which may affect an individual's emotional and social wellbeing		37
	2.3 Outline the effects of ageing in the later stages of life		38–39
E3 CFC7 Eating healthily	**1. Know the importance of eating healthily.**	3	44–45, 47
	1.1 List the main food groups.		44–45
	1.2 State why it is important to eat food from each of the main food groups.		44–45
	2. Know about combining food to make up a balanced diet.		46–47
	2.1 List the foods which form a balanced diet for the following meals: a) morning – breakfast b) mid-day – main meal c) evening – tea.		46
L1 CFC20 Healthy eating for families	**1. Understand the importance of a balanced diet.**	3	48–49, 56
	1.1 List the main food groups.		48
	1.2 State what is meant by a balanced diet		48
	1.3 State the effects of a balanced diet on health		49
	2. Know about good eating habits for families.		50–51, 56
	2.1 Outline the importance of family mealtimes		50
	2.2 Describe ways to encourage children to eat healthily		51
	2.3 Identify a healthy meal for children		51
	3. Know special food requirements for groups and individuals.		52–53, 57

Unit	Learning outcome	Page
	2.1. List ways the adult can support a young child's play in the home.	118
	2.2. Identify the responsibilities of the adult during a young child's play in the home	119
	1. Know how children learn.	122–23, 130
	1.1. Identify ways that children can learn.	122–23
	1.2. Outline ways that children use senses to find out about the world.	123
	1.3. Outline ways that children use senses to find out about the world.	123
	2. Know how to use stories and rhymes with young children.	124–25, 130–31
L1 CFC13 Sharing learning experiences with children	2.1 Identify stories and rhymes for children 0-5 years	124
	2.2 Identify sensory aids to support children's enjoyment of stories	124
	2.3 State way to encourage children to take part in stories or rhymes	125
	3. Understand that the natural world can support children's learning.	126–27, 130–31
	3.1 Identify objects of interest from the natural world	126
	3.2 List natural environments which may be used to extend children's experiences	126–27
	3.3 Give an example of how outdoor experiences can develop children's curiosity	127
	4. Know how the local community can be used to broaden children's experiences.	128–31
	4.1 List local organisations, services or people that can provide experiences for children	128
	4.2 State the benefits of finding out about the local community for children	128
	4.3 Give examples of ways that local organisations, services or people working in the community can broaden children's experiences	129
	1. Know how babies' development is supported by play.	132–35, 146
	1.1 State ways that babies' development is supported by play in the following areas: Physical Social and emotional Intellectual and language	132–35
	1.2 Give examples of how the individual needs of babies can be supported through play	135
	2. Know about play activities for babies.	136–43, 146–47
L1 CFC17 Supporting babies to play	2.1 Identify different play activities and the resources to support play for the following ages: a) Babies from birth to 3 months b) Babies from 4 to 7 months c) Babies from 8 to 11 months d) Babies from 12 to 15 months	136–42
	2.2 State what the benefits are to babies of each play activity identified	143
	3. Know the role of the adult in providing play for babies	144–47
	3.1 Identify the adult's role in ensuring that babies can play safely	144
	3.2 Give examples of how adults encourage babies to play	145
	1. Understand the features of a positive learning environment.	148–51, 162–63
L1 Understanding play for early learning	1.1 Identify features of a setting that contribute to a positive learning environment.	148–51
	1.2. State how these features might help children to learn.	148–51
	2. Understand how play can help children's learning or development.	152–59, 163
	2.1. Outline some ways in which play can help children's learning in each of the following: a) physical, b) social, c) emotional development, d) intellectual, e) language.	152–59

Unit	Learning outcome	Chapter	Pages
	3. Understand that play and activities should meet individual needs and avoid stereotyping and discrimination.		160–61, 163
	3.1. Suggest how a given set of materials, resources or activities might reinforce or challenge stereotyping and discrimination.		160–61
L1 CFC21 Science activities for young children	1. Know science activities suitable for young children.		166–71, 172
	1.1 List science activities suitable for children aged: a) 18 months to 2 years b) 3 years to 5 years.		168–71
	1.2 Describe a science activity for each age range.		166–71
	2. Know how to set up science activities to support the young child's learning.	8	168–73
	2.1. List the resources needed to carry out the science activity for each age range.		168–71
	2.2. Identify the possible health and safety risks for the listed science activities.		168–71
	2.3. Identify the support a child may need when carrying out the science activities previously listed.		168–71
	3. Know the learning which young children can gain from science activities.		168–71, 173
	3.1. Identify what would be the expected learning for the child in each activity listed.		168–71
L1 CFC23 Musical activities for young children	1. Know the benefits of musical activities for young children.		174–79, 182–82
	1.1. List musical activities suitable for the following aged children: a) babies under 6 months b) young children 1 to 2 years c) young children 3 to 5 years.		174–79
	1.2 Identify the benefits for the child for each activity listed.		174–179
	2. Know how to make musical activities or musical games for young children.	8	180–81, 183
	2.1. Describe how to make a musical activity or musical game for young children.		180–81
	2.2. Identify the value to young children of chosen musical activity or musical game.		180–81
	2.3. Identify the learning that could take place for young children taking part in chosen musical activity or musical game.		180–81
E3 CFC8 Contraception information	1. Know about contraception.		186–187, 190–91
	1.1 List methods of contraception.		186–187
	1.2 State the strengths and weaknesses of each method of contraception listed.		186–187
	2. Know where to seek advice in relation to contraception.	9	188–189, 191
	2.1 Identify where support on contraception can be obtained.		188
	2.2. Give examples of professionals available to talk to individuals about contraception.		189
E3 CFC6 Responsibilities of new parent(s)	1. Know about a baby's growth and development during pregnancy.		192–93, 198
	1.1 State the stages from conception to birth.		192–93
	2. Understand the care required for a mum during pregnancy.	9	194–95, 199
	2.1. Identify how a mum-to-be should care for herself before the birth of her baby.		194
	2.2. List factors which could harm an unborn baby.		195
	3. Know the support available to new parent(s).		196–97, 199
	3.1. List support that new parent(s) may need during the first 12 weeks of a baby's life.		196–97
	3.2. Identify where to obtain support for: a) the new baby b) the new mum c) the new parent(s).		197

Introduction

This chapter covers:

E3 IRRE3 Individual rights and responsibilities

Rights are very often discussed, but not easily understood, in relation to children. Chapter 1 sets out to explain what rights mean, how they differ from rules, and what morals we hold ourselves and why these are important.

Learners need to understand that there are rights enshrined in law such as the Human Rights Act (1998) and the United Nations Convention on the Rights of the Child (1989). However, in reality, sometimes one person's rights might directly conflict with another person's rights and so an individual's responsibility becomes important.

Throughout this chapter learners will gain a better understanding of their responsibilities within society.

Having an awareness of their own rights will enable learners to be better able to consider the rights of others.

Learning outcomes

Unit IRRE3

Unit IRRE3 has one learning outcome:

1. Understand that they have individual rights and responsibilities.

Teacher checklist

✓ What are morals and why are they important?

✓ What is the difference between rules and rights?

✓ What laws help to uphold rights?

✓ What rights do we have for ourselves?

✓ What responsibilities do we have to others?

Learners should reflect upon their responsibilities throughout each unit that they study. There are strong links between this unit and CFC9 Respecting and valuing children.

Additional guidance for delivery

You might like to question learners about what influenced their moral decision in Activity 1.A1 and whether when they could visualise a person being connected to the £5 note, they felt differently about it.

Obtaining a child-friendly version of the United Nations Convention on the Rights of the Child (1989) is helpful when discussing what rights children have (see Further resources below).

This unit will include lively debate and conversation, so a starting activity could be to introduce an agreement for constructive argument.

Empowering young people to understand what rights they have can also lead them to challenge set rules. A constructive way to deal with this could be to direct learners to Unit CFC9 Activity 6.A8 and to begin to plan their proposal as outlined.

As a group, or on an individual basis, ask the learners to complete the interactive **Knowledge check** to finish the chapter.

Further resources

www.direct.gov.uk

This website is a useful and accurate source for learners to find out more about their rights, and how they can better exercise them.

www.crae.org.uk

This is a good resource for tutors and also includes an under 18s section, thus making it accessible for young people.

www.unicef.org.uk

Child-friendly versions of the United Nations Convention on the Rights of the Child (1989) are available to download along with resources for tutors and interactive games and quizzes for children and young people.

www.rights4me.org

This is the website of the Children's Rights Director for England and deals with the rights of children who are living away from home, for example in a boarding school or children's home. It contains lots of helpful information for adults and children.

Shackell, Butler, Doyle and Ball (2008) *Design for Play: A Guide to Creating Successful Play Spaces*, Department for Children, Schools and Families.

This is a very appealing book, outlining successful play space projects around the country. Its use of colourful photographs makes it accessible for children and young people.

Answers to activities

1.A6

13 years
- Have a part-time job

16 years
- Have a full-time job
- Get married with parents' consent
- Buy a lottery ticket or scratch card

17 years
- Hold a drivers licence
- Donate blood

18 years
- Change name
- Place a bet
- Have a tattoo
- Buy or drink alcohol

Chapter 1 Your rights and responsibilities

Overview of resources

Resources	Teaching notes	Link to Student Book	Link to Units and assessment criteria
1.A1 The £5 note dilemma	Before beginning this activity you might like to introduce the concept of 'morals' (the principle of right and wrong). This activity allows the learner to explore their own moral code through a scenario of finding a £5 note. This could be read aloud by the tutor or given out in groups. The idea is that you build up the dilemma in stages with learners pondering each point before proceeding to the next. It is best delivered in groups or as a whole class activity where learners can contribute via lively discussion and debate.	p.5	**IRRE3** *AC 1.4*
1.A2 Rules and rights	It is important that learners appreciate the difference between 'rules' and 'rights'. Rules are something imposed by others whereas rights are something we hold ourselves. The activity will help learners to think about turning rules into rights. This might mean that they have to consider others' rights as well as their own. An example has been given to help learners to get started. This could be a group or individual activity. The following activity (1.A3) is a development of this activity.	p.4	**IRRE3** *AC 1.3, 1.4*
1.A3 Our rights	Carrying on from the previous activity, the learners will now consider rights that they have. (At this point you might like to introduce the United Nations Convention on the Rights of the Child (1989).) You could direct your learners to investigate this themselves using ICT. Every young person in the UK has the right to an education: Articles 28 and 29 of the UNCRC discuss this right. In this activity learners will explore their class/group rights. They must consider the rights of the learners and the rights of the tutor. This activity could be treated with great importance, and used to form a set of class rights that all must sign and agree to. It is important that this process is done democratically to ensure that all learners feel valued and involved in the process. This is an individual, small group and whole group activity.	p.2–5	**IRRE3** *AC 1.1, 1.3, 1.4*

Resources	Teaching notes	Link to Student Book	Link to Units and assessment criteria
1.A4 The noisy neighbours **1.H1** The Human Rights Act (1998)	The Human Rights Act (1998) impacts upon life and death matters but also the basic everyday rights that we often take for granted. In order to set a background to this activity, allow learners to read through the basic set of rights covered by the Act (1.H1).	p.4–5	**IRRE3** AC 1.1, 1.3, 1.4
	In small groups learners should read the scenario of the 'noisy neighbours' presented in Activity 1.A4. In their groups they should decide which side they agree with. They should then develop an argument using the Human Rights Act (1998) as support for their argument and then constructively debate the argument. They should then attempt to find a resolution to the situation that is agreeable to both parties.		
	This activity will help the learners to understand that rights are not straightforward, and being responsible can be challenging at times.		
1.A5 Article 31	Thinking back to The United Nations Convention on the Rights of the Child (1989), one Article that is sometimes overlooked is Article 31.		**IRRE3** AC 1.1, 1.2
	This states that children (those under the age of 18) have the right to rest and play.		
	This is interesting because children in their middle and later years have very little public space to actively engage in play. You might like to introduce this subject by discussing: What is play?; How do older children play? You should ask what your learners think about 'No ball games' signs in parks and how older children might play in public spaces.		
	This activity enables learners to think about their educational environment and to design a space that might be used for rest and play. They should also reflect upon a public space known to them such as a shopping centre or local park. They should design an area here to enable rest and play. The focus should be upon positive engagement not antisocial behaviour (you might like to reinforce this by referring to the Human Rights Act (1998) and responsibility to others).		
	This is an individual activity. You could develop it to include studies of local areas, or development of plans and materials.		
1.A6 At what age can I...?	This activity is to reinforce what rights learners have.		**IRRE3** AC 1.1
	Learners look at the set of rights and highlight what they believe to be relevant to them at their age.		
	Learners then reflect upon whether they believe the age ranges are right, and make suggestions for other rights and amendments to ages.		
	This activity is an individual activity with group discussion.		

Resources	Teaching notes	Link to Student Book	Link to Units and assessment criteria
Electronic resources			
1.PPT Individual rights and responsibilities	This PowerPoint presentation summarises the differences between morals, rules and rights. It outlines the laws that affect us and our responsibilities to others. These are the topics that will be covered in this unit and will introduce learners to the areas for discussion and further investigation.		
Knowledge Check	Interactive quiz covering learning from the units in the chapter for consolidation purposes. You could run the quiz via the VLE with learners during the first session to see how much they already know; it could be done again later to see how much progress they have made. Alternatively, more independent learners could have a go at completing the quiz on their own.		

1.A1 The £5 note dilemma

Consider the scenario below.

You have just had to pay a huge bill and have only a couple of pounds left in your bank account. It is your mother's birthday and you cannot even afford to buy her a card.

You are walking home when…

- You find a five pound note being blown in the wind. You bend down to pick it up – no one around seems to notice or to have dropped it.
  So… do you keep it?

- What if, instead of being blown down the road, the five pound note was in a blank envelope, on the floor outside a post office?
  Do you keep it now?

- But what if the five pound note is inside a wallet? There is nothing else except the five pound note. No details, no address and no identity to trace the owner. It is still outside the post office, lying on the floor. Everyone else is ignoring it.
  Do you keep the money now and, if you do, what do you do with the wallet?

- Now imagine that the wallet contains a photograph of a child. There is also a receipt from a pet shop for two tins of cat food.
  What now? Will you keep the money? If so, what will you do with the photograph and the wallet?

- The wallet containing the five pound note is handmade. There is a picture of a child and a small scribbled drawing saying, 'I love you Nanny'. There are bank cards and a bus pass containing the photograph of an elderly lady whose name appears to be Violet Grey.
  What are you going to do now? Will you keep the money or hand in the wallet?

The scenario above is what we call a 'moral dilemma'; what you decide to do is based upon your own moral judgement.

1.A2 Rules and rights

Rules are made by other people. Rights are things that we own ourselves. All of us have rights in all areas of our lives.

1. Look at the following set of rules and turn them into rights. The first one has been completed to help you get started.

Rules	Rights
Do not talk when the teacher is talking	*Everyone has the right to listen and be heard*
No bullying	
Glass not allowed in play park	
No swearing	
No filming or taking photographs	
No smoking	

2. Can you now make a rule from this right?

Rights	Rules
To be able to sit quietly and study in the library	

1.A3 Our rights

It is important that as a class or group, every learner is aware of their own responsibilities in the learning environment.

1. In the first column of the table, record your expectations or 'rights' as a learner. In the second column consider what rights your tutor has within the learning environment. An example has been given for you.

Your rights as a learner	Your tutor's rights
To have well prepared and interesting lessons	*To be respected by learners*

2. Now you have thought carefully about the rights within the learning environment, discuss your responses in a group. Decide upon the six that you feel are the most important.

3. Make sure that you have good reasons for thinking that these rights are important because you need to propose that these rights be adopted for the class. Jot down some ideas to help you.

4. In a class, vote upon a set of agreed rights for everyone. You could decide that these should be made more official by getting everyone in the class to sign that they agree to them.

1.A4 The noisy neighbours

Jason and Albert are neighbours.

It is a lovely warm sunny Sunday afternoon.

It is also the semi-final of the World Cup and England look like they might actually win this time.

It is also a year to the day that Albert's wife, Judith, passed away.

Jason's story

Jason loves football. When he was little all he ever wanted was to be a footballer.

Now he is 28 years old, married to Sue and living in a house that is too small. He does a job he hates and his only pleasure in life is watching football on television.

He has become so excited by the thought that England might win the World Cup that he has painted his house and decorated his garden ready for a barbecue with all his friends. They have moved the television into the garden and are singing and chanting loudly.

Albert's Story

Albert is 78. He is lonely and feels isolated.

He moved into his house with his dear wife, Judith, who passed away suddenly last year.

He has planned to sit in the garden and remember Judith by playing her favourite songs (loudly because he is hard of hearing).

Albert does not like football and is not aware that today is such an important day for football fans.

As you can imagine, each neighbour wants to enjoy the sunny weather in their garden.

Each is annoyed by the other's noise and an argument breaks out.

1. Decide who you feel is in the right, and why you think this is.

2. In groups, plan your argument. You need to have a clear idea of why you think your argument is right. (You could use the Human Rights Act (1998) to support your argument – see 1.H1.)

3. Finally, as a group decide upon a peaceful resolution to this situation.

1.A5 Article 31

'All children have the right to rest and play, and join in with a wide range of activities.'

The United Nations Convention on the Rights of the Child (1989)

Think about this right.

1. Do you feel that there is an area where you can rest and play in your educational environment?

2. If money and space were no object, how would you design a rest and play space?

   Be creative with your design; include things to engage males and females and you should also think about those with disabilities. You could use:

   - drawings
   - photographs
   - bullet points
   - diagrams
   - lists
   - video
   - ICT.

3. Now think about a public space you know well – it could be a shopping centre or park. Design a space that would allow you to rest and play. It is important that you remember your responsibilities to others, so your play must not upset anyone else.

   You might like to think about natural environments and materials such as wood, ropes and trees.

1.A6 At what age can I...?

Below is a list of rights that young people have.

1. Read through it and decide what rights you believe you have at your age. Highlight these by using a highlighter pen or drawing a circle around them.

- Change your name
- Have a tattoo
- Have a part-time job
- Get married with parents' consent
- Buy or drink alcohol

- Donate blood
- Buy a lottery ticket or scratch card
- Hold a driving licence
- Have a full-time job
- Place a bet

2. Now you have been told the answers, are you surprised?

3. Are there any rights you feel you should have but do not have at your age?

4. Are there any rights for which you would change the ages?

1.H1 The Human Rights Act (1998)

You have the responsibility to respect other people's rights, and they must respect yours.

Your human rights are:

- the right to life
- freedom from torture and degrading treatment
- freedom from slavery and forced labour
- the right to liberty
- the right to a fair trial
- the right not to be punished for something that was not a crime when you did it
- the right to respect for private and family life
- freedom of thought, conscience and religion, and freedom to express your beliefs
- freedom of expression
- freedom of assembly and association
- the right to marry and to start a family
- the right not to be discriminated against in respect of these rights and freedoms
- the right to peaceful enjoyment of your property
- the right to an education
- the right to participate in free elections
- the right not to be subjected to the death penalty.

1. Are there any rights that you think are wrong?

2. Why do you think this is?

Introduction

This chapter covers:

L1 CFC14 Growth and development of young children

L1 CFC15 Human growth and development

Chapter 2 brings together Units CFC14 and CFC15, focusing on the patterns and areas of growth and development from birth to old age. Learners need to understand that while development should be viewed in a holistic manner, breaking it down into separate areas can help with understanding developmental norms.

It is important that learners understand how social, cultural and religious influences affect how we view the ageing process.

The newborn infant is born with many abilities, and learners need to appreciate the diverse capabilities of individuals from the newborn through to the adult in older age.

Activities also focus upon the positive and negative influences upon growth exploring disability, diet and inherited conditions.

Learning outcomes

Unit CFC14

Unit CFC14 is divided into two learning outcomes:

1. Know about factors which influence growth and development of children from birth to 5 years 11 months.

2. Know how to support growth and development of children.

Teacher checklist
- ✓ Understand that development usually happens in a set pattern
- ✓ Know what is meant by developmental norms
- ✓ Know the difference between environmental and genetic influences upon development
- ✓ Development happens in physical, intellectual, emotional and social areas
- ✓ Children need to be supported in each area of development in order to lead active and healthy lives
- ✓ Understand the impact of social and cultural differences upon development

Unit CFC15

Unit CFC15 is divided into two learning outcomes:

1. Know about human growth and development

2. Know factors which affect human growth and development

Teacher checklist
- ✓ Understand that development usually happens in a set pattern
- ✓ Know what is meant by developmental norms
- ✓ Know how the body ages with time
- ✓ Understand how life events affect development

These units underpin much of the learning of this course. Learners will notice links between CFC14 learning outcome 1 and HL1 learning outcome 1.

Additional guidance for delivery

It is a good idea for learners to use the developmental timeline (see Activity 1.A1) as a resource for note taking, building upon information to use as a point of reference.

Learners should be given the opportunity to explore different concepts of childhood, including concepts from countries other than the UK, for example those in the developing world. It is also important to reflect upon how older age is viewed in society, especially by the media. Examining the differing values placed upon older age in different cultures and religions where elder members of society are viewed as having greater wisdom and experience will extend learners' knowledge of diversity.

As a group, or on an individual basis, ask the learners to complete the interactive **Knowledge check** to finish the chapter.

Further resources

www.ageuk.org.uk

Helpful website containing information related to those in their later years; includes information about rights and current topics.

Department for Children Schools and Families (2008) *Practice Guidance for the Early Years Foundation Stage* DCSF Publications, Nottingham

Development expectations for children from birth to 5 years are mapped out in this document. Development is broken down into six areas of learning. It might be advisable to edit the information for relevance to learners' needs and understanding.

www.majorityworld.com

A useful website for obtaining real life images of people in the Majority World. It contains photographs to purchase taken by indigenous photographers. These could be used as part of discussion and reflection upon differences in expectations of human growth and development.

Meggitt (2007), *An Illustrated Guide to Child Development,* Heinemann, Oxford

This bright and colourful illustrated guide presents childhood development in easy to follow photographic order. It is well suited to learners of all levels and provides a breakdown of each area of development for each age range.

www.nhs.uk/tools/pages/birthtofive.aspx

A useful guide to child development including video and audio materials.

Answers to activities

2.A2

Match left boxes to right as follows:

- 1 = f
- 2 = e
- 3 = b
- 4 = d
- 5 = g
- 6 = a
- 7 = c

Chapter 2 Human growth and development

Overview of resources

Resources	Teaching notes	Link to Student Book	Link to Units and assessment criteria
2.A1 Sequencing life stages	This activity is designed to give learners a starting point for thinking about growth and development. Learners could build upon the resource they make in this activity to gather notes and use as a point of reference. (Ensure A3 size paper is given.) Learners cut out each image and arrange in order, then label each life stage underneath. As an extension activity, learners could estimate an age range for each.	p.28–33	**CFC15** AC 1.1
2.A2 Developmental milestones for young children	Learners now need to focus upon children from birth to 5 years and 11 months of age. Learners will match developmental milestones to the correct age range. They should then examine the factors described in each case study and suggest what milestone may be delayed in each case. It is important to stress that developmental norms provide only an approximate guide.	p.10–17	**CFC14** AC 1.1, 1.2
2.A3 What influences growth and development?	Learners are to explore what factors influence growth and development. These have been separated into the following categories: environmental and genetic. Learners should be reminded of equality and diversity and different practices towards childrearing. Learners are to look at the factors influencing growth and development and the children discussed in the final section. They should suggest: *What has affected development* and *Why this might have affected growth and development.*	p.18–19 p.36–37	**CFC14** AC 1.2 **CFC15** AC 2.1
2.A4 Vital statistics	This is a practical activity. You will require tape measures, a flight of stairs and a mirror. In this activity learners are to think about their own growth and development. They will record and compare their data to that of another student. This activity will reinforce the variation of rates of growth and development. Extension tasks could include analysing their results and suggesting influencing factors.		**CFC14** AC 1.2 **CFC15** AC 2.1
2.H1 PIES	It is important that learners understand that growth and development happens in different areas, and how these are all interlinked. The handout sheet includes an explanation of development in physical, intellectual, emotional and social areas. Learners could use this information to suggest development for each person on their timeline completed in Activity 2.A1. If this is not possible, they might like to consider their own development in each area and what factors have affected this.	p.34–35	**CFC15** AC 1.2

Resources	Teaching notes	Link to Student Book	Link to Units and assessment criteria
2.A5 Let's get active!	This activity will help learners to think about children being fit and active, contributing to a healthy lifestyle. Learners design two simple playground games or activities using a selection of suggested resources. An extension activity could be to describe the benefit of the activities designed. This could be completed individually or as a small group.	p.20–21 p.22–23	**CFC14** AC 1.3, 2.1
2.A6 Say what? **2.H2** Cards for 2.A6	This is a pair or small group activity. This is an activity to encourage learners to think about communication and language. In doing so it will also create opportunities for social development. You might like to ask learners to reflect upon the social aspects within groups or individually. To create the cards used in each of the games, you will need to use 2.H2 Handout 2.H2 is designed to be copied and cut out and could be backed on card or laminated to make it more hardwearing. The cards are used to play the games described on Activity 2.A6.	p.24–25	**CFC14** AC 2.2, 2.3
2.A7 The busy nursery **2.H1** PIES	Learners will gain an awareness of how children develop in different areas. This activity will introduce the concept that some toys and play opportunities promote development in specific areas. Learners are to look at the different areas of the nursery and suggest what areas of development might be encouraged in each. The information on handout 2.H1 will be useful for this activity.	p.22–25	**CFC14** AC 2.1, 2.2, 2.3
2.A8 Life events	When considering life events, it is important to stress the existence of cultural and social differences. Learners are to complete the table of life events by suggesting how it might feel, and how they might interact with others at this time. It is important to stress that in this activity there are no right or wrong answers. Sensitivity is required for discussing this topic. This is an individual activity that can then be shared in small or large groups.	p.37–39	**CFC15** AC 2.2, 2.3
2.A9 Verity is getting older	This activity is about exploring the effects of older age. It is very important that you stress that ageing is universal, but responses to it are vastly different according to differing cultures. This activity could be carried out in large scale as a whole group. Learners need to use their own body to discuss what happens to each area as the body gets older.	p.38–39	**CFC15** AC 2.3

Resources	Teaching notes	Link to Student Book	Link to Units and assessment criteria
Electronic resources			
2.PPT Human growth and development	This PowerPoint presentation introduces learners to the idea of stages and patterns of development from birth to old age, the areas of development, how life events affect us and how the body ages as we get older. These topics will be discussed in more detail in this chapter.		
Knowledge Check	Interactive quiz covering learning from the units in the chapter for consolidation purposes. You could run the quiz via the VLE with learners during the first session to see how much they already know; it could be done again later to see how much progress they have made. Alternatively, more independent learners could have a go at completing the quiz on their own.		

2.A1 Sequencing life stages

Cut out the images and the headings below and rearrange them into the correct life order. You could then stick them on to another sheet of paper.

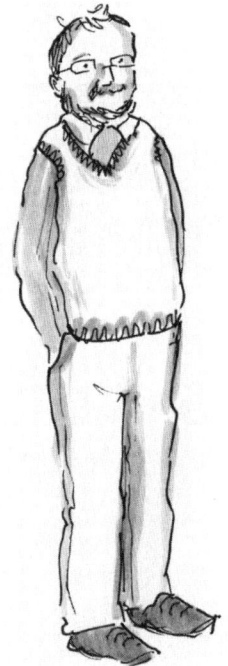

Babyhood	Adolescence	Older age	Childhood
	Adulthood		

2.A2 Developmental milestones for young children

Remember, developmental milestones are just a guide of what we expect children to be able to do.

1. Match the developmental milestone to the approximate age at which this occurs.

Milestone	Approximate age
1. Begins to crawl	a. 16 months old
2. Begins to use two or three words in a sentence when talking	b. Birth
3. Can grasp finger if placed in hand	c. 5 years old
4. Will be able to eat skilfully using a fork	d. 4 years
5. Can count up to ten	e. 2 years old
6. Can walk unaided	f. 9 months old
7. Will be able to read basic stories for themselves	g. 3 years old

2. Now look at each scenario below and suggest what milestones might be delayed for each child.

A

Kathryn is 18 months old. She has had three operations on her hip, and has had her legs in plaster for six months.

> Milestones that might be delayed…

B

Adam has just started school. He has visual difficulties and can only see blurred shapes.

> Milestones that might be delayed…

2.A3 What influences growth and development?

Some things affect our development and our growth, either for better or worse.

We call these 'factors'. Below are some factors that influence our growth and development.

Environmental factors

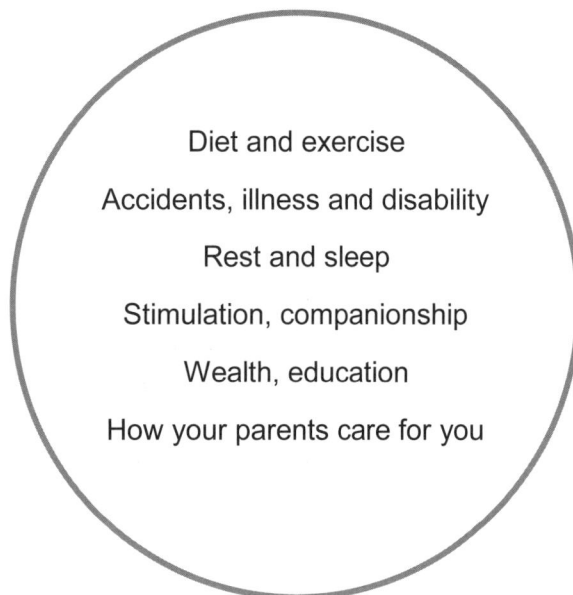

Diet and exercise

Accidents, illness and disability

Rest and sleep

Stimulation, companionship

Wealth, education

How your parents care for you

Genetic factors

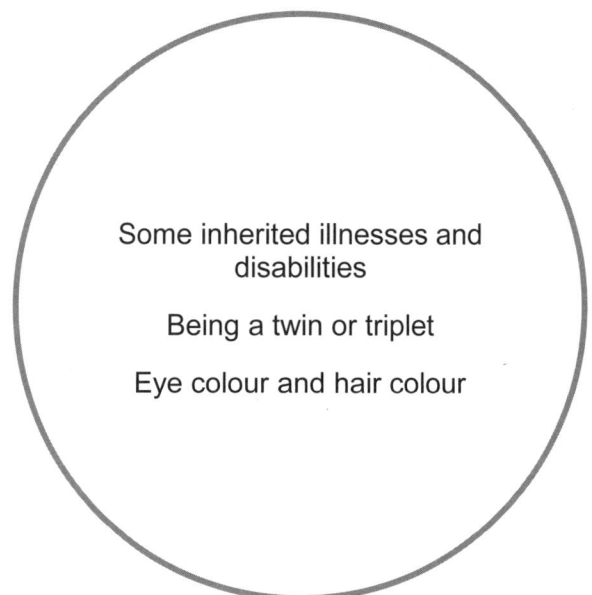

Some inherited illnesses and disabilities

Being a twin or triplet

Eye colour and hair colour

Read the two descriptions below and then fill in the table

A Ismail is a twin. He was very small because he was premature when he was born, and has some learning difficulties.

B Hannah lives in a large house with a big garden. She eats lots of fresh fruit and vegetables. She attends ballet classes, swimming lessons and also goes for long walks with her parents each Sunday.

Child	What has affected their growth and development?	Why might their growth and development be affected?
Ismail		
Hannah		

2.A4 Vital statistics

1. In pairs, measure and record your personal data below. Compare your data with your partner.

Height	Shoe size	Hand span
You: Partner:	You: Partner:	You: Partner:

Your height, shoe size and hand span are largely influenced by **genetic** factors. But can you think how **environmental** factors might affect them too?

2. Now let's think about other things affected by environmental factors.

Number of stairs run up before being out of breath	Number of teeth with fillings	Number of hours you slept last night
You: Partner:	You: Partner:	You: Partner:

What might affect each of these results?

2.A5 Let's get active!

It is really important that young children get lots of opportunity to have physical exercise every day.

1. Imagine that you are a play ranger. Your job is to go into primary schools and encourage young children to be more active during playtime. You have brought some resources with you.

Small and large balls	Bamboo canes
Skipping ropes	A large parachute
Tunnels	Cloth sacks
Hula hoops	2 metres of thick elastic
Tyres	A plank of wood
Bean bags	

In the playground are some natural items you could also use:

Trees and tree stumps	A sand pit	A grassy area

Now you must design at least two games or activities to help children to get active and fit. Describe the ideas you come up with.

Activity 1

Activity 2

2.A6 Say what?

You will have some cards to use for each of these games. You will use the same cards for each game.

1. **Who am I?**
   - One person (the guesser) takes a card from the pile without looking at it. This card is either stuck on the wall above their head (without them being able to see it) or could be shown to their partner or the rest of the group and then placed back in the pack.
   - The guesser is allowed to ask five questions to the partner or group, but they can only respond with yes or no. An example of a question could be: *Am I furry?*
   - At the end of the five questions the guesser needs to say what animal they think they are.

2. **Back to back drawing**
   - Two people sit in chairs with their backs to each other. One person chooses two cards and the second person has a sheet of paper and pencil. The person with the cards needs to give instructions of how to draw the animal they have on each card. They must not say what the animal is, and they must not use words such as snout or beak.
   - At the end the drawer will compare their drawing to the card. If it doesn't look the same, whose fault is it – the drawer or the instruction giver?

3. **Describe me**
   - One person selects a card and has to describe the animal on the card to the rest of the group. They must not use any noises the animal makes or say its name.
   - You could time yourself to see how many you get through in a minute.

4. **Act out**
   - This is an activity a bit like charades. One person picks out a card and must do ONE action of that animal that will enable the partner or group to guess what the animal is.
   - The person must not speak at all during their action or the guessing.

5. **Signing**
   - In your group or pair, you need to devise a form of sign language for each animal. Think carefully about how you might do this, because each sign for each animal should be different and unique.
   - When you have practised, join with another group or pair and see if you can guess each other's animals.

These games are great for practising your skills in questioning, describing, body language, repetition, memory, logical thinking and guessing.

2.A7 The busy nursery

Busy Nursery has lots of activities set out for the children.

1. Using your knowledge of development in different areas – physical, intellectual, emotional and social (PIES) – write down what development might be promoted by each activity below?

Play dough	
Role play kitchen	
Jigsaw puzzles	
Bikes	
Dolls and puppets	
Building bricks	
Scissors and paper	
Group games	

2. Ben loves to play with the jigsaw puzzles at nursery. He also likes to use building bricks to make castles. What area is Ben developing?

3. Stanley likes to run around the nursery with his three friends. Stanley is always with other children and does not like to play alone. What area is Stanley developing?

2.A8 Life events

Read through each life event and decide the emotions someone might feel at the time, and how they might interact with others at the time. The first one has been completed to help you.

Life event	Emotions felt	Interactions with others
Starting school	Anxious, scared, excited, nervous	Meeting others the same age and getting to know the teacher
Leaving home to go to university		
Starting first job		
Falling in love		
Getting married		
Having a baby		
Getting divorced		
Life partner dying		
Moving into care home		

CFC15
A.C. 2.3

2.A9 Verity is getting older

1. Verity is celebrating her 80th birthday. Identify how Verity might have aged using the areas suggested.

Hair

Mind

Voice

Skin

Bones

Height

Internal organs

2. How might Verity feel?

3. How do you feel about Verity?

2.H1 PIES

Development can be separated into four main areas.

These are:

- Physical
- Intellectual
- Emotional
- Social

We can remember these by using the acronym **PIES**.

You might like to shade each pie in a different colour to help remember the differences.

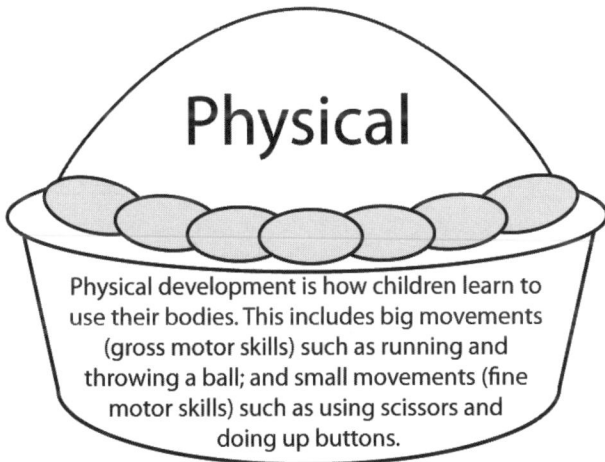

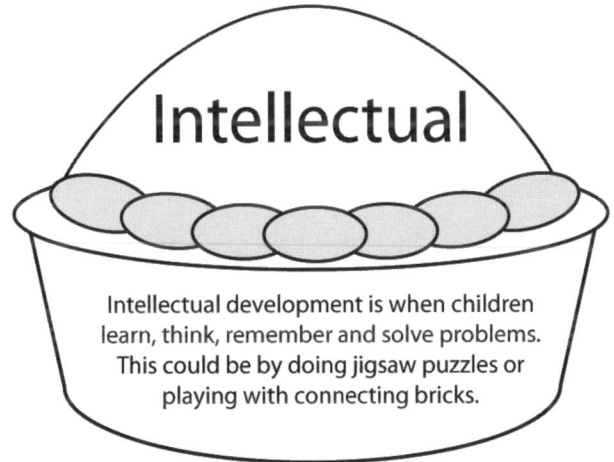

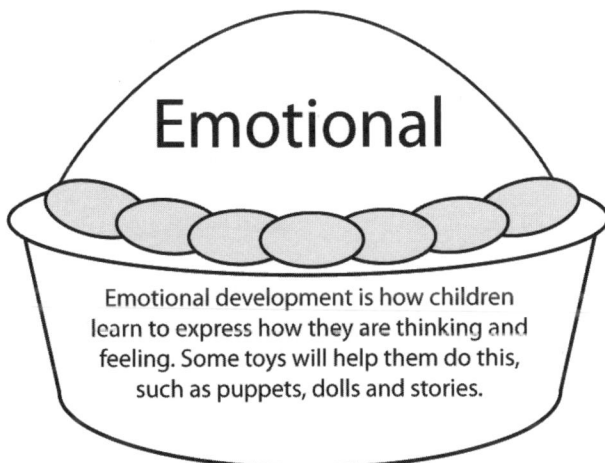

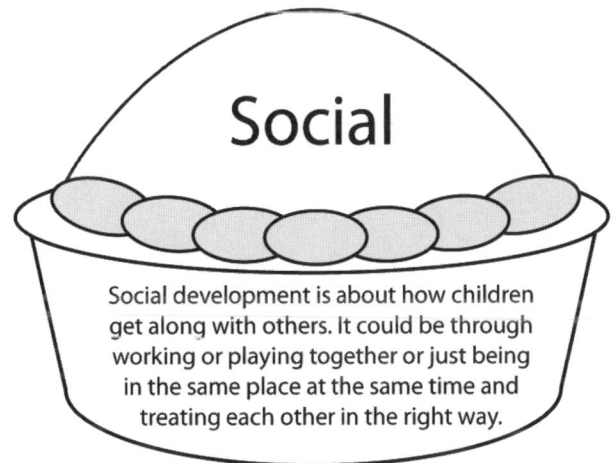

Physical

Physical development is how children learn to use their bodies. This includes big movements (gross motor skills) such as running and throwing a ball; and small movements (fine motor skills) such as using scissors and doing up buttons.

Intellectual

Intellectual development is when children learn, think, remember and solve problems. This could be by doing jigsaw puzzles or playing with connecting bricks.

Emotional

Emotional development is how children learn to express how they are thinking and feeling. Some toys will help them do this, such as puppets, dolls and stories.

Social

Social development is about how children get along with others. It could be through working or playing together or just being in the same place at the same time and treating each other in the right way.

2.H2 Cards for 2.A6

These drawings could be stuck on card and laminated.

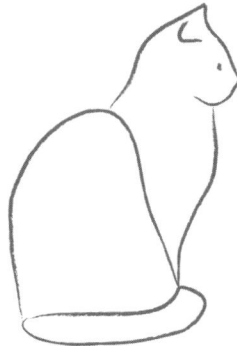

Introduction

This chapter covers:

E3 Unit CFC7 Eating Healthily

L1 Unit CFC20 Healthy Eating for Families

L1 Unit HL1 Healthy living

Healthy living and eating are important and relevant to everyone; those working with children have the added responsibility of needing to be good role models. This chapter looks at the learners' own health and well-being as well as that of children.

A healthy attitude towards food, along with knowledge of portion size, what a balanced diet consists of and how to enjoy family meals together will enable learners to make healthy choices when eating.

The chapter provides the opportunity for reflection upon food requirements of different faiths and cultures and identification of foods that might cause allergic reactions. This information is essential to all those who have contact with young children in order to treat those with differing needs respectfully. Learners will develop an understanding of safe food handling practice and will explore the risk of cross-contamination, an understanding of which is essential for food safety. They will also learn about management of special diets.

Greater understanding of where they can make improvements in their own lives will enable learners to become healthier.

Learning outcomes

Unit CFC7

Unit CFC7 has two learning outcomes

1. Know the importance of eating healthily
2. Know about combining food to make up a balanced diet.

> **Teacher Checklist**
> ✓ What nutrients are contained in different foods
> ✓ The different food groups
> ✓ Correct portion size

Unit CFC20

Unit CFC20 is divided into four learning outcomes:

1. Understand the importance of a balanced diet
2. Know about good eating habits for families
3. Know special food requirements for groups and individuals
4. Know how to handle and store food safely

> **Teacher Checklist**
> ✓ How to combine foods to make a balanced diet
> ✓ The benefits for children eating together as a family
> ✓ Special diets for different religious and cultural groups
> ✓ Common foods that cause allergies
> ✓ Risks of cross-contamination in food handling
> ✓ Good hygiene in food preparation

Unit HL1

Unit HL1 is divided into three learning outcomes:

1. Understand the importance of leading a healthy lifestyle.
2. Demonstrate how they contribute to own healthy lifestyle.
3. Review the activities undertaken to maintain a healthy lifestyle.

Teacher Checklist
- ✓ The importance of a balanced diet
- ✓ Eating the right portion size
- ✓ Factors that promote a healthy lifestyle
- ✓ Positive factors that influence wellbeing

Additional guidance for delivery

Activity A4 requires learners to undertake some individual research and so access to library facilities is helpful.

There is a wealth of conflicting advice within the media and via product advertising as to what constitutes a healthy choice in food. This could be discussed as a class using food labels and advertisements as a talking point. Learners might also examine how food is marketed to children and whether healthy options are as prominent as less healthy choices.

Discussion around food restrictions and requirements could be made more accessible to learners by including taste sessions and guest speakers to explain the reasons behind the special considerations with food.

An active session could see learners assessing the food safety within a fridge (for example in a staff room) or studying the effects of deterioration of foods by keeping food past its use-by date for observation.

As a group, or on an individual basis, ask the learners to complete the interactive **Knowledge check** to finish the chapter.

Further resources

www.cwt.org.uk

www.cwt-chew.org.uk

The Catherine Walker Trust provides information about nutrition and healthy eating, including current research and advice. The Children Eating Well (CHEW) campaign provides information about healthy and balanced foods for children.

www.faithandfood.com

Provides information about the dietary requirement of different faiths.

www.food.gov.uk

The Food Standards Agency provides information about all food matters from nutrition to safety and hygiene.

www.jamieoliver.com

The much publicised TV chef outlines his campaign for better school dinners including his manifesto for better standards in children's food served at school.

Answers to activities

3.A1

1.

Breakfast	Lunch	Dinner	Snacks and drinks
Leah, 6 years old			
• Brown toast *carbohydrate* • Butter *fat* • Milk *calcium*	• Tuna sandwich *protein, fluoride* • Kiwi fruit *vitamin C* • Crisps *fat*	• Chicken *protein* • Potatoes *carbohydrate* • baked beans *vitamin B* • Rice pudding *calcium, vitamin D*	• Banana *carbohydrate* • Water *fluoride* • Bar of plain chocolate *iron*
Isla, 2 years old			
• Wheat cereal *vitamin E* • Orange juice *vitamin C*	• Bread sticks *carbohydrate* • Slice of cheese *fat, calcium, vitamin D* • Grapes *vitamin C* • Yoghurt *vitamin D, calcium*	• Beef bolognaise *protein, iron* • pasta *carbohydrate* • mushrooms *vitamin B* • green beans *vitamin K* • Custard *protein, vitamin A*	• Milk *calcium, vitamin E* • Water *fluoride* • Orange *vitamin C* • Ice cream *fat*
Muhira, 4 years old			
• Boiled egg *protein* • Toast *carbohydrate*	• Packet of crisps *fat*	• Pizza with cheese and tomato *carbohydrate, fat, vitamin B* • Fruit salad *vitamin C*	• Cola *no nutritional value* • Bar of milk chocolate *fat* • Apricots *vitamin A*

2.

Child	Missing food groups
Leah	Vitamin A and K could be improved by eating more green vegetables. Spinach would also provide more iron.
Isla	There is something from all nutrient groups
Muhira	This is quite a poor diet. There needs to be more iron and Vitamins D, E and K. Eating more fresh green vegetables would improve the diet.

3.A4

- Fish, eggs, meat – protein – helps the body resist infection and disease…
- Fruit, vegetables – vitamins – helps to build cells...
- Milk, cheese – calcium – helps to build strong teeth…
- Cooking oil, oily fish – fats – provides the body with energy when resting...
- Bread, pasta, potatoes – carbohydrates – broken down into glucose...
- Water, diluted juice – water – main component of cells and blood...
- Green vegetables – iron – helps to produce oxygen-carrying...

3.A7 Q2

- prawns – shellfish
- yoghurt – milk
- mayonnaise – eggs
- bread – wheat
- peanut butter – nuts

Chapter 3 Healthy living

Overview of resources

Resources	Teaching notes	Link to Student Book	Link to Units and assessment criteria
3.H1 Nutrients in common foods **3.A1** Fussy eaters	In order to understand what constitutes a balanced diet it is important that learners know what nutrients are contained within different foods. Handout 3.H1 will help them to do this and could be retained for use with further activities. Activity 3.A1 should be used together with 3.H1. Learners will work individually or in groups to look at each case study and decide whether or not each child is eating foods from all of the food groups.	p.44–45 p.48–49	**CFC7** AC 1.1 **CFC20** AC 1.1, 1.2, 2.3
3.A2 What is a balanced diet? **3.A3** Portion size	Learners need to consider what they ate the previous day. Learners examine the recommendation of a balanced diet according to the pie chart. Using the blank diagram, learners record their own intake and consider whether or not it is balanced. This could also be used to consider whether the children in 3.A1 had eaten a balanced diet on the day recorded. Activity 3.A3 encourages learners to think about portion size and can be used to help them consider suitably sized meals for children and themselves. It will help them to consider whether they are eating enough of each food group.	p.48–49	**CFC7** AC 1.2, 2.1 **HL1** AC 1.1
3.A4 A healthy diet	Learners should be directed to research what each type of nutrient does for the body. This information is needed to complete Activity 3.A4. The activity explores how the body uses each nutrient. You could discuss how some diets (such as cutting out carbohydrates) are bad for the body.	p.44–45 p.49	**CFC7** AC 1.2 **CFC20** AC 1.3
3.A5 Good eating habits	Family mealtimes provide an opportunity for young children to learn good eating habits. With the increase in both parents working and the availability of readymade meals, many children end up sitting in front of the television to eat their dinner. This activity focuses on busy family life and how it impacts upon eating habits. Learners have the opportunity to discuss these habits and recommend changes and then design tableware that would liven up their dinner table.	p.50–51	**CFC20** AC 2.1, 2.2

Resources	Teaching notes	Link to Student Book	Link to Units and assessment criteria			
3.H2 Special dietary requirements **3.A6** Dinner is served	Learners will understand that different religious and cultural groups require special consideration with their diet. Handout A.H2 outlines some of these, and should be used to complete Activity 3.A6. This activity asks the learner to create suitable breakfast, lunch and dinner menus for three children, considering their special requirements.	p.52–53	**CFC20** AC 3.1, 3.2			
3.A7 Food allergies	It is essential that learners are aware of the seriousness of food allergies. Activity 3.A7 outlines common foods that might cause allergies and asks learners to consider cross contamination and why the factors mentioned are important. Lastly, learners need to think about what foods are unsuitable for allergy sufferers. This could be a group or individual task.	p.53 p.55	**CFC20** AC 3.3, 4.3			
3.H3 Basic food hygiene **3.A8** Frankie's kitchen	Hand washing is essential to maintain hygienic practices. Learners also need to be aware of safe storage and preparation of foods. Handout 3.H3 describes the basics of good food hygiene. Using this information, learners will address the issues in Frankie's kitchen (Activity 3.A8). This activity provides many opportunities for learners to express their knowledge and can be differentiated by guiding able learners to complete the whole sheet. Less able learners can complete just the bottom half.	p.54–55	**CFC20** AC 4.1, 4.2			
3.A9 Alex's day	Learners look at a day in the life of Alex. This demonstrates small things that contribute towards a healthy lifestyle such as exercise, personal hygiene, socialising, eating a balanced diet and getting enough sleep. Learners need to identify the positives. More able learners could try to identify why these are beneficial, or class discussion could take place. Learners could then record their own typical Saturday and make comparisons, identifying changes they could implement.	p.58–63	**HL1** AC 1.1, 1.2			
Electronic resources						
3.PPT Healthy living	This PowerPoint presentation will introduce learners to the main topics of discussion covered in this unit such as food groups, nutrients found in foods, restricted diets and managing food hygiene.					
Knowledge Check	Interactive quiz covering learning from the units in the chapter for consolidation purposes. You could run the quiz via the VLE with learners during the first session to see how much they already know; it could be done again later to see how much progress they have made. Alternatively, more independent learners could have a go at completing the quiz on their own.					

3.A1 Fussy eaters

Some parents are worried about their children's eating habits.

1. Read through the daily food sheet for each child and work out what food groups each item belongs to and what nutrients it contains.

Breakfast	Lunch	Dinner	Snacks and drinks
Leah, 6 years old			
• Brown toast and butter • Glass of milk	• Tuna sandwich • Kiwi fruit • Crisps	• Chicken, potatoes, baked beans • Rice pudding	• Banana • Water • Bar of plain chocolate
Isla, 2 years old			
• Wheat cereal • Orange juice	• Bread sticks • Slice of cheese • Grapes • Yoghurt	• Beef bolognaise with extra mushrooms, pasta and green beans • Custard	• Milk • Water • Orange • Ice cream
Muhira, 4 years old			
• Boiled egg and toast	• Packet of crisps	• Pizza with cheese and tomato • Fruit salad	• Cola • Bar of milk chocolate • Apricots

2. Do the children have any food groups or nutrients missing from their diet?

Child	Missing food groups
Leah	
Isla	
Muhira	

3.A2 What is a balanced diet?

1. Look at the diagram below. It shows the balance of foods to help aid a healthy lifestyle.

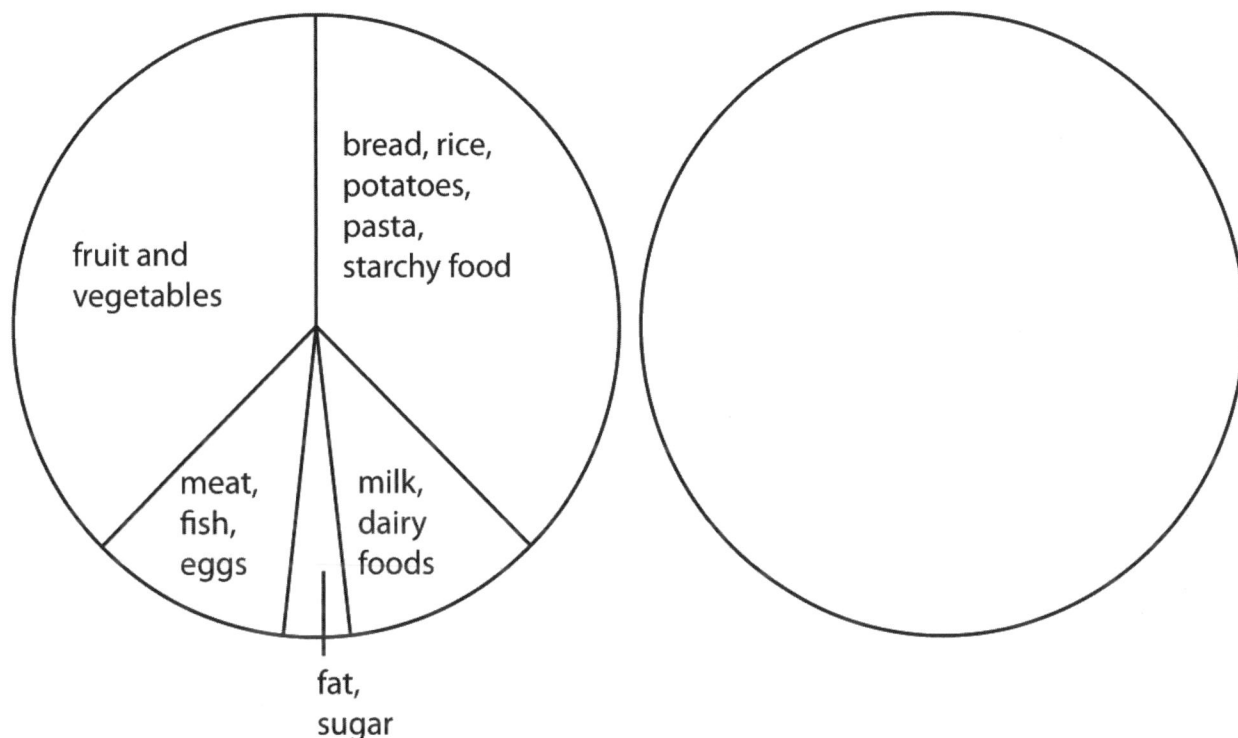

fruit and vegetables

bread, rice, potatoes, pasta, starchy food

meat, fish, eggs

milk, dairy foods

fat, sugar

2. Now complete the empty pie chart above, showing the balance of foods you ate yesterday. Is it healthy?

3. What foods could you eat at each meal time to improve your diet?

Breakfast	
Lunch	
Dinner	

3.A3 Portion size

There is a quick and easy way to assess whether you are eating the correct portion size. You should use the palm of your hand as a guide. If the portion of food fits within your palm, it is correct.

1. Below is the outline of a 3-year-old child's hand. Using the foods listed below, estimate the correct portion size for the child (for example – one small banana).

2. Now draw around your own hand on a blank sheet of paper and estimate portion sizes of the foods listed below for yourself.

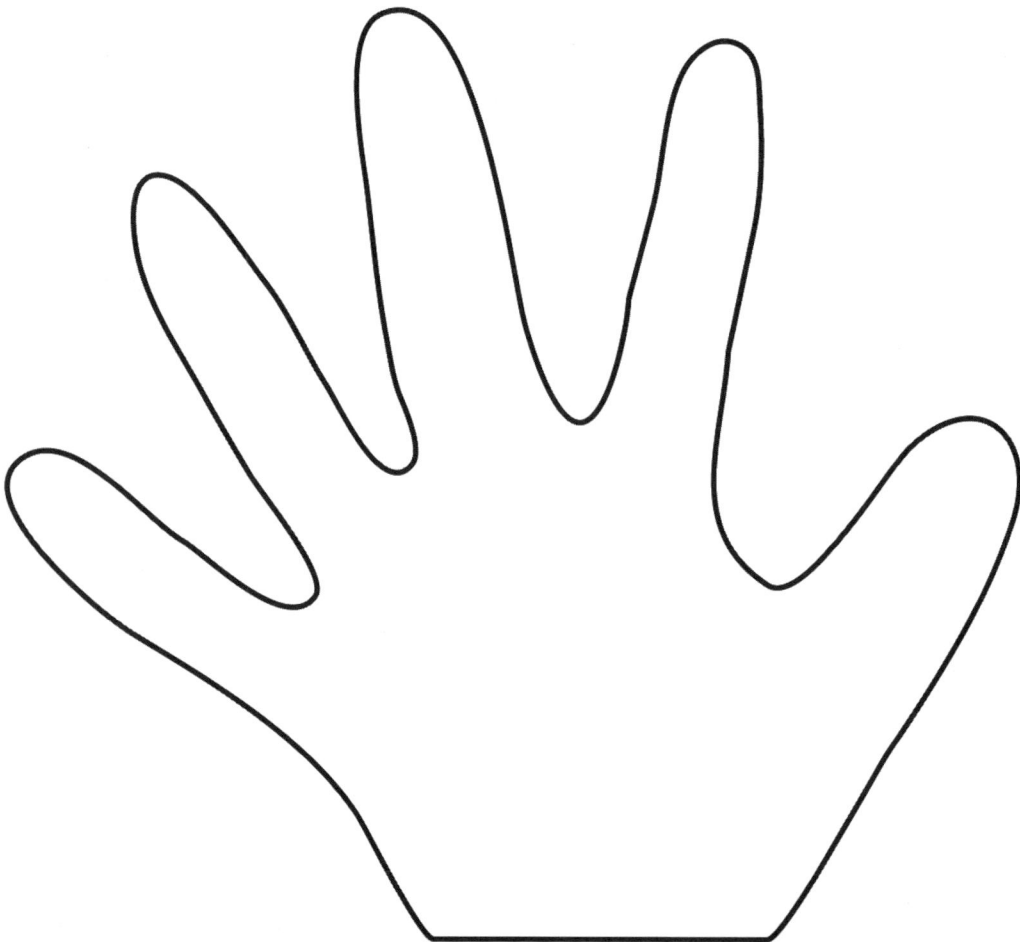

banana	sausages	chicken
potatoes	chips	broccoli
ham	boiled eggs	pasta
bread	ice cream	tomatoes
grapes	biscuits	orange
apples	beans	

3.A4 A healthy diet

1. Link the food type to the nutrient and then the way that the body uses the nutrient. An example has been given for you.

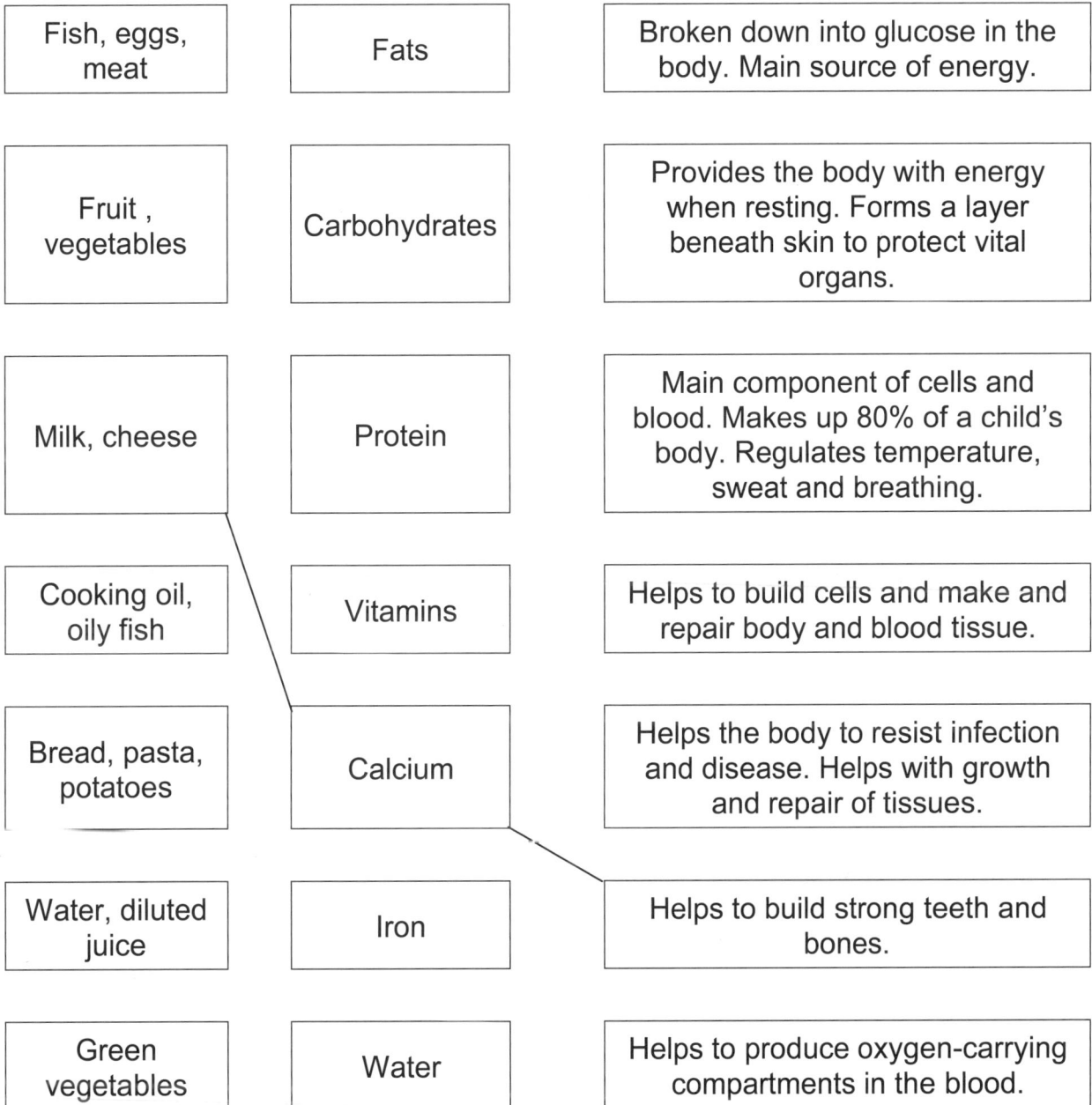

Fish, eggs, meat		Fats		Broken down into glucose in the body. Main source of energy.
Fruit , vegetables		Carbohydrates		Provides the body with energy when resting. Forms a layer beneath skin to protect vital organs.
Milk, cheese		Protein		Main component of cells and blood. Makes up 80% of a child's body. Regulates temperature, sweat and breathing.
Cooking oil, oily fish		Vitamins		Helps to build cells and make and repair body and blood tissue.
Bread, pasta, potatoes		Calcium		Helps the body to resist infection and disease. Helps with growth and repair of tissues.
Water, diluted juice		Iron		Helps to build strong teeth and bones.
Green vegetables		Water		Helps to produce oxygen-carrying compartments in the blood.

CFC20

A.C. 2.1, 2.2

3.A5 Good eating habits

The Smith family are all very busy.

Every day Mum drops off the youngest child, Betty, at nursery on her way to work. Dad leaves the house at 6 a.m. and does not return from work until after 8 p.m. Emilie is 16; on her way to school she buys a hot sausage roll from the local bakery for lunch. Tom is 13 and he eats a packet of mini cereal from the box on his walk to school. Tom is the only one in the family who eats breakfast other than Betty who has breakfast at nursery.

In the evening Mum picks Betty up and gives her a jar of baby food while she does the housework.

Dad eats a microwave dinner when he gets in at about 8.30 p.m. Emilie gets herself and Tom dinner; usually it is a burger or chips from the local shops because they both like to go out with their friends after school.

1. What three things could the Smith family do to improve the way they eat?

   a.

   b.

   c.

2. How might this improve things for everyone?

3. Think about making the dinner table look more appealing. Design some tableware such as napkins, plates, cups and glasses that will brighten up the dinner table. Be as creative as you like!

3.A6 Dinner is served

In this activity you will consider the diet of three children. You need to create a suitable breakfast, lunch and dinner for each.

1. Anil is a Sikh. He isn't keen on vegetables and does not like pizza. Anil needs to take a packed lunch to school with him.

Breakfast	
Lunch	
Dinner	

2. Imtiaaz is a strict vegan. He has a big appetite and needs to eat his main meal at lunchtime.

Breakfast	
Lunch	
Dinner	

3. Shola is Rastafarian. She would like to go out with friends after school. Can you suggest a suitable location for dinner as well as a suitable meal?

Breakfast	
Lunch	
Dinner	

3.A7 Food allergies

Food allergies can be very serious. They can range from the sufferer experiencing unpleasant symptoms such as stomach cramps to serious cases resulting in anaphylactic shock and death.

Below are some of the most common food allergies:

- nuts
- shellfish
- milk
- eggs
- wheat
- fish
- soya
- seeds

1. Here is some 'good practice' advice for avoiding cross contamination of foods. Explain why this is important when someone has a food allergy.

Good practice	Why this is important
Having separate cooking utensils, chopping boards and other equipment	
Washing hands thoroughly	
Using clearly labelled storage boxes	
Changing cooking oil with each use	

2. Link the allergy to the unsuitable food type.

milk		prawns
shellfish		yoghurt
nuts		mayonnaise
wheat		bread
eggs		peanut butter

3.A8 Frankie's kitchen

Frankie has his young nephew coming to stay. He needs to sort out his kitchen and make it safe for food preparation. He says standards have 'slipped' a bit.

1. Can you identify some of the hazards in the descriptions of the kitchen and the picture below?
2. Suggest why they are dangerous.
3. Explain how to put them right.

You might like to set out your answer like this. (An example has been done for you.)

Hazard	Why it is dangerous	How to put it right
There is no hot water	Hands and equipment need to be washed in hot water to remove germs.	Get the tap fixed. Use water boiled in the kettle (but cooled down) until it works.

In Frankie's kitchen:

- Jasper the cat sleeps on the work surface
- the hot tap does not work
- there is no soap or washing up liquid
- there are flies buzzing around a plate of cooked sausages

- there is only one wooden chopping board
- there are spills over the work surface
- there is only one one sharp knife
- the tea towel is wet and dirty.

Frankie's fridge

a piece of uncooked beef

last night's left-over chicken

broken hinge

temperature 10°C

mouldy cheese

the fussy cat's dinner

a wilted carrot

something spilt

fresh milk and 'on the turn' milk

3½ cans of lager

half-finished antibiotics

a fresh lemon

3.A9 Alex's day

This is a typical Saturday for Alex.

8.30 a.m. *Excellent!! An hour longer in bed, then cooked breakfast.*
9.30 a.m. *Football training at the leisure centre with friends.*
11.00 a.m. *Get showered and changed.*
12.30 p.m. *Go to town with Mum, get hair cut and eat jacket potato and salad lunch.*
2.30 p.m. *Dad picks me up. Walk dogs in woods and have a shandy in pub.*
4.00 p.m. *Go to grandparents with Dad, play Scrabble (again!).*
6.30 p.m. *Back home for a roast dinner. Watch television for an hour.*
7.30 p.m. *Go to friend's house, play on dance mat and chat.*
9.30 p.m. *Get a lift home, early night because feeling tired.*

1. Do you feel that Alex has a healthy lifestyle?

2. List factors that positively contribute towards Alex's well-being under the following headings. An example has been given for you

Diet	Exercise	Rest	Play	Social interaction	Personal hygiene
		An extra hour in bed means he is well rested			

3. What factors could negatively affect Alex's well-being?

3.H1 Nutrients in common foods

Nutrient	Found in
Carbohydrate	Bread, pasta, flour, potatoes, bananas, vegetables
Protein	Meat, eggs, fish, milk
Fat	Butter, margarine, vegetable oil, meat, fish and dairy products
Vitamin A	Carrots, milk, apricot, fatty fish, margarine
Vitamin B	Bread, meat, yeast, pasta, flour, rice, noodles
Vitamin C	Oranges, lemons, grapefruit, kiwi fruit
Vitamin D	Milk, margarine, cheese, yoghurt
Vitamin E	Vegetable oil, green leafy vegetables, milk, nuts and wheatgerm
Vitamin K	Most vegetables
Iron	Red meat, broccoli, spinach, plain chocolate
Calcium	Milk, cheese, butter, yoghurt
Fluoride	Tap water and sea fish

3.H2 Special dietary requirements

People might eat a special diet because they follow a particular religion or have a cultural or personal belief (such as not wanting to eat animals).

Below are some special dietary requirements.

Group	Restriction	Details
Hindus	Do not eat beef or beef products	Many Hindus will be vegetarian. Some may eat fish but not meat. Eggs might also be excluded from diet. Spend a period of time fasting.
Jews	Do not eat pork or pork products	Meat eaten by Jews needs to be prepared in a special way and will need to be 'kosher' certified. They will only eat fish with fins and scales. Preparation of food is important. Meat and dairy are not eaten together and should not be prepared together. Separate utensils must be used for each.
Muslims	Do not eat pork and pork products	Special preparation of meat is required making it 'Halal'. No shellfish is eaten. Spend a period of time fasting.
Sikhs	Do not eat beef or beef products	Will not eat meat that is 'kosher' or 'halal'. May have vegetarian diet.
Rastafarians	Do not eat animal products except milk	No chemicals should be used in foods and canned foods are usually avoided. Food should be raw if possible. Do not drink coffee.
Vegetarians	Do not eat meat or meat products	Most avoid gelatine and animal fats.
Vegans	Do not eat meat or dairy or eggs	Will avoid all animal products including honey.
Pescetarians	Do not eat meat	Will eat fish and may eat other animal products.

It is important to remember that each person is an individual and may observe different dietary rules. Always check exactly what their requirements are, and show the utmost respect at all times.

This is especially important when working with young children who will be unable to explain that they do not eat certain things, or may be unaware of its content in meals and snacks.

3.H3 Basic food hygiene

Below are some general guidelines for keeping food preparation safe and hygienic.

1. **Always** wash and dry hands thoroughly before preparing food. This should be in clean, hot, running water using a liquid soap. You should dry your hands with disposable towels.
2. Check **use by** dates on food. This is a guide for when the food should be eaten by.
3. Clean up any spills immediately.
4. Dishcloths can spread germs. It is important that they are not left damp because germs multiply in damp warm conditions. The best method of wiping up spills is using disposable cloths.
5. Tea towels can also harbour germs. To keep the risk down tea towels should be changed every day. Ideally use disposable cloths to dry up.

Some germs such as E. coli and salmonella are found in certain foods. However, they can be killed by thorough cooking. Here are some general rules to follow:

- Always follow the instructions on the label for cooking times
- Always check your food is piping hot in the middle – there should be steam coming out
- Don't reheat food more than once
- When reheating, take extra care your food is cooked all the way through.

Storing food correctly in a fridge will help reduce the risk from germs. Here are a few useful things to remember:
- Keep the fridge at the right temperature (about 5°C)
- Keep the fridge door closed – do not leave it open unless you are taking food out. Close it quickly afterwards
- Wait for food to cool down before you put it in the fridge

When preparing and storing food always remember to:
- keep raw meat separate from ready-to-eat food
- do not let raw meat drip blood or juices onto other food – it is safest to keep it in a sealed container at the bottom of the fridge
- never use the same chopping board for raw meat and ready-to-eat food.

Introduction

This chapter covers:

E3 CFC3 Providing a safe and hygienic environment for a young child

L1 CFC24 Practical health and safety when with young children

It is important that new and inexperienced practitioners understand that health and safety should not limit children's enjoyment of their environment, nor prevent well supervised trips to local areas.

This chapter enables learners to consider forward planning and identification of potential risks in order to overcome them. It also identifies the child's own role in risk management and safety.

Identifying ill health in children can help to prevent infection spreading and so learners will develop an awareness of the signs and symptoms of ill health. Accompanying prevention of ill health is the identification of personal hygiene routines that contribute towards well-being. Learners need to understand their own responsibilities in relation to hygiene as well as supporting the management of children's routines.

Learning outcomes

Unit CFC3

Unit CFC3 has three learning outcomes:

1. Know the importance of personal hygiene.
2. Know about signs of ill health in a young child.
3. Know about keeping a young child safe in the home.

> **Teacher checklist**
> ✓ Which routines help to promote good personal hygiene
> ✓ Care routines to promote children's personal hygiene
> ✓ Symptoms of serious ill health
> ✓ Symptoms of less serious ill health
> ✓ How to respond to children who are unwell
> ✓ Safety measures to ensure children's safety
> ✓ Garden hazards and how to reduce them

Unit CFC24

Unit CFC24 has three learning outcomes:

1. Know about health and safety guidelines and instructions.
2. Know about health and safety equipment which helps to keep children safe.
3. Know about fire safety when with young children.

Teacher checklist

✓ How and why household products are labelled

✓ The common labels found on products

✓ Identification of safety labels on toys

✓ Where and how safety products might be used in the home

✓ What equipment can be used to help prevent accidents

✓ What poses a risk of fire in the home

✓ How to reduce the risk of fire

✓ What resources can be used to prevent or alert the presence of fire

Additional guidance for delivery

It is important that learners are aware that some signs of ill health are a medical emergency in young children. Learners should be directed that 'if in doubt' a medical professional's opinion must be sought.

This could form part of a discussion about making an emergency 999 call and what information would be required.

As a practical exercise to accompany Activity 4.A3, learners could practise hand washing and investigate different items available to assist with this. The use of alcohol gel could also be discussed.

To support safety within the home, learners could use catalogues to find safety equipment suitable for the home of the grandparents discussed in Activity 4.A6.

A guest speaker from the local fire service would help to introduce learners to the risks of fire within the home, linking to fire safety.

As a group, or on an individual basis, ask the learners to complete the interactive **Knowledge check** to finish the chapter.

Further resources

www.capt.org.uk

The Children's Accident Prevention Trust provides common sense ideas for keeping children safe and also has statistical information about accidents involving children.

http://firekills.direct.gov.uk/index.html

Includes information about what to do in the event of a fire and useful information about how to prevent fires from starting in the first place.

www.hse.gov.uk

The Health and Safety Executive contains downloadable leaflets and information relating to a wide variety of safety issues.

www.rospa.com

The Royal Society for the Prevention of Accidents provides a wealth of information about accidents involving children in and outside of the home.

Answers to activities

4.A1

2.

- Cutting finger nails – weekly – to keep underneath nails clean
- Brushing teeth – at least twice a day – to keep them clean and prevent decay
- Washing hair – every few days – to keep clean and reduce tangles
- Bathing – every few days – to wash whole body and for relaxation
- Changing nappy – when it is dirty or every four hours – to prevent nappy rash and to keep the baby comfortable
- Washing hands – regular intervals – always before eating to prevent spread of germs
- Brushing hair – at least daily – to prevent tangles and check for lice

4.A2

Minor

- Being quiet – observe the child for further symptoms
- Not wanting to eat – continue to offer food
- Feeling sleepy – encourage to sleep and monitor
- Being grizzly – offer comfort and be patient
- Wanting comfort – offer comfort and be patient
- Flushed cheeks – take temperature
- Rubbing ears – check for discharge, see a doctor
- Shivering – keep child warm and monitor

Serious

- Being floppy – seek urgent medical attention (could be an indication of loss of consciousness)
- Having a rash that does not disappear under a glass – call an ambulance immediately (could be a sign of meningitis)
- Very high temperature – keep cool, give plenty of fluids, give paracetamol as directed and seek urgent medical attention
- High-pitched cry – seek urgent medical attention (could be indication of pain)

4.A7

- Broken fence
- Neighbour's cat
- Steep steps,
- Broken greenhouse glass
- Sharp tools
- Rotting rubbish
- Uneven paving slabs
- Pond
- Holes around tree

Chapter 4 Keeping children healthy and safe

Overview of resources

Resources	Teaching notes	Link to Student Book	Link to Units and assessment criteria
4.A1 Personal hygiene	Learners will reflect upon their own personal hygiene routine, and the frequency of activities. They will then consider the differences for young children and reflect upon why each is important.	p.68–69	**CFC3** AC 1.1, 1.2
4.A2 Feeling unwell	Learners will look at signs of ill health in children and categorise these as minor or serious. They will then link suggested responses to each sign of ill health. This would work well as a group activity. You should tell learners that some signs might require more than one response, or may have the same response.	p.70–71	**CFC3** AC 2.1, 2.2
4.A3 Caring for Munir	This activity will help learners to think about what might be wrong with the child who is unwell. Information is included in the top half of the activity sheet for learners to use for question 1. You might like to guide learners to conduct some independent research to build on their knowledge of the chosen illness.	p.70–71	**CFC3** AC 2.1, 2.2
4.A4 Health promotion	Learners need to link the way in which hygienic practices can help to prevent ill health and disease from spreading. Activities 4.A4 and 4.A5 will help learners to think about how these two concepts link together. There are opportunities for practical extensions on both activities, which could include presentations, making leaflets and posters.		**CFC3** AC 1.1, 1.2, 2.1, 2.2
4.A5 Farmyard bugs	This case study centres on a school trip to a farm which results in the children becoming unwell. It looks at the importance of hand washing before eating and cleaning wounds properly. Learners need to identify the cause of illness, the treatment to be given and also discuss what might have prevented the children from becoming unwell.	p.68–71	**CFC3** AC 1.1, 1.2, 2.1, 2.2
4.A6 Staying with grandparents	This activity will help learners to think about safety within the home. Learners will consider the safety of a grandparent's home for two young children. Suggesting safety items that may be required, such as cupboard locks and stair gates, will help learners to consider risk management.	p.72–73 p.78	**CFC3** AC 3.1, 3.2 **CFC24** AC 2.1, 2.2

Resources	Teaching notes	Link to Student Book	Link to Units and assessment criteria
4.A7 Garden safety	Continuing on from Activity 4.A6, this task considers safety in the garden. The learners should think about potential hazards and could be prompted to explain why the item is dangerous. Learners should explain ways of making the garden safer. Stress that there might be uncontrollable risks such as the neighbour's cat. At this point it might be helpful to introduce the idea that children need to manage some risks for themselves.		**CFC3** *AC 3.1, 3.2* **CFC24** *AC 2.1, 2.2*
4.H1 Safety guidance and labelling	This handout contains information about safety guidance and labelling on children's toys and equipment. This will enable learners to answer the questions asked in Activity 4.A8. Learners will explain why the toys grandfather has got for the children might be unsafe.	p.76	**CFC24** *AC 1.1*
4.A8 Grandfather's toys			
4.H2 Symbols on household products	Understanding what symbols mean on household products is important to maintain safety. Learners can use this handout to find out more about these symbols and some general guidance on using cleaning products. This information can then be used to explain the dangers in each scenario in Activity 4.A9.	p.76	**CFC24** *AC 1.2*
4.A9 Cleaning around the house			
4.A10 Taking Tom and Ellis out	Learners will investigate the importance of forward planning when taking small children out of the house. This activity will lead them to consider the safety aspects of short trips. It reminds the learner that children need to take some responsibility for their actions and by setting agreed rules before leaving the house, children know what is expected of them.	p.77 p.79	**CFC24** *AC 1.3, 2.3*
4.A11 Fire safety	Activity 4.A11 will help learners to understand the risk posed by fire. It is important to stress the importance of modelling behaviour that ensures safety when with young children. Learners could use this activity as a foundation for a wall display, or short project.	p.80–81	**CFC24** *AC 3.1, 3.2, 3.3*

Resources	Teaching notes	Link to Student Book	Link to Units and assessment criteria
Electronic resources			
4.PPT Keeping children healthy and safe	This PowerPoint presentation provides a brief overview of the important issues relating to keeping children safe and healthy. Learners will be introduced to topics such as personal hygiene routines and labelling of household products that are covered in this unit.		
Knowledge Check	Interactive quiz covering learning from the units in the chapter for consolidation purposes. You could run the quiz via the VLE with learners during the first session to see how much they already know; it could be done again later to see how much progress they have made. Alternatively, more independent learners could have a go at completing the quiz on their own.		

4.A1 Personal hygiene

Personal hygiene is very important whatever your age.

1. Think about the routines you have for maintaining your own personal hygiene and how often you do these things. Make notes in the table below.

Activity	How often you do this	Reasons
Washing hair	*Every other day*	*To stop it getting greasy*

2. Now consider a young child's personal hygiene and fill in the gaps in the table.

Activity	How often this should be done	Reasons
Cutting fingernails		To help keep underneath nails clean
	At least twice a day	To keep them clean and prevent decay
Washing hair		
	Every few days	
	Whenever it is dirty or every four hours	To prevent a rash from forming, and to make the baby more comfortable
Washing hands		
		To prevent tangles and check for head lice

4.A2 Feeling unwell

1. Below are some signs children might show when they are unwell. Decide whether these are minor (not serious) signs or serious signs of ill health. Use the first two columns to write your answers.

    - Being quiet
    - Not wanting to eat
    - Being floppy
    - Feeling sleepy
    - Being grizzly
    - Having a rash that does not disappear under a glass

    - Wanting comfort
    - Flushed cheeks
    - Very high temperature
    - Shivering
    - Rubbing ears
    - High-pitched cry

Minor	Serious	Suitable response

2. In the third column of the table write the most suitable response to each sign, choosing from the list below.

    - Give paracetamol as directed
    - Keep child warm and monitor
    - Continue to offer food
    - Give plenty of fluids
    - See a doctor
    - Offer comfort and be patient

    - Take temperature
    - Seek urgent medical attention
    - Check for discharge
    - Call an ambulance immediately
    - Encourage to sleep and monitor
    - Keep cool

4.A3 Caring for Munir

Read through these signs and symptoms of ill health in young children.

Illness	Sign and symptoms	Treatment
Chicken pox	• Fever, tiredness, sore throat and aching before spots appear. • Red flat spots that appear all over body and are very itchy. These then turn into a blister and crust over.	• Give plenty of fluids. • Discourage scratching. • Add a small amount of oatmeal or bicarbonate of soda to a tepid bath for the child. • Comfort.
Diarrhoea	• Urgency in needing to open bowels. • Stomach ache. • Very loose stool.	• Give plenty of fluids to prevent dehydration. • Change nappy more frequently or allow child to use potty when needed. • Comfort.
Conjunctivitis	• Sticky eyes with yellow discharge. • Child may rub eyes. • Eyes look red and sore.	• Eye drops are required from the doctor. • Careful cleaning of eyes using cotton wool and cooled boiled water. • Distract child from rubbing eyes. • Comfort.
Tonsillitis	• Sore throat with difficulty swallowing. • May have high temperature and headache.	• Under direction, paracetamol could be given. • Give plenty of fluids. • Soups and yoghurts might be easier to eat. • Encourage rest. • Comfort.

1. Imagine that you are helping to care for Munir for the day because he is unwell. He is 3 years old and will be at home. First, you need to select one of the common illnesses from the table above.

2. Suggest a daily plan of care that includes:
   • the foods and drinks you will offer
   • activities to keep him amused
   • how you will monitor the illness
   • what treatment you might need to give.

4.A4 Health promotion

1. Imagine that you are a health promotion worker. You have been asked to go into a school to talk to children and their parents. You will talk about **head lice** or **thread worms**.

   You will need to plan an 'awareness day' that will include activities and information for both children and adults. You should include information about prevention, how the condition is spread and how it is treated.

   You need to be sensitive, because some children and parents are embarrassed and need reassurance that these conditions are common and not their fault.

   You might like to use

   - posters
   - leaflets
   - PowerPoint presentations
   - crosswords
   - games
   - drama
   - photographs
   - wall displays
   - table displays
   - artwork
   - short film
   - cartoons
   - puppet show
   - treasure hunt

2. You need to encourage the school to prevent the spread of other conditions. You notice that there are no tissues available, no soap for hand washing and the children eat their meals at their school desks without them being wiped over first.

   Write a simple plan for improvements the school could make. They have a budget of £1000 for this purpose, so you can suggest some items they might need to purchase.

   You must also think about helping the children to understand hygiene better, so your plan needs to get them involved too.

4.A5 Farmyard bugs

Class 4B visited an open farm to learn more about animals.

- During the trip one of the children (Danielle) tripped over and grazed her knee when running to see the baby goats.
- Another child (Fergus) was bitten by a lamb, but after running his hand under the tap for a few minutes he felt OK.
- The children all ate their packed lunches at the picnic tables in a barn except two children (Meena and Wendy), who went home early because they were in the school choir.
- All of the children played in the sand and cuddled rabbits in the barn when it started to rain.

The following day lots of children were absent from school. Their symptoms included stomach aches, diarrhoea, sickness, headaches, a sore swollen leg and high temperature.

Wendy, Meena and Fergus came to school as usual and were not unwell.

1. What do you think has made the children unwell?

2. How might they need to be cared for while they are feeling unwell?

3. Why do you think Meena, Wendy and Fergus are not unwell?

4. What do you think could have prevented the children from becoming unwell?

4.A6 Staying with grandparents

Matthew (3 years old) and Alan (1 year old) are going to stay at their grandparents' house for the weekend.

Their grandparents are trying to think about all the possible dangers and what they can do to make the house more child-friendly.

1. Below is a plan of the different rooms in their house. You need to identify potential dangers for Matthew and Alan in each room.

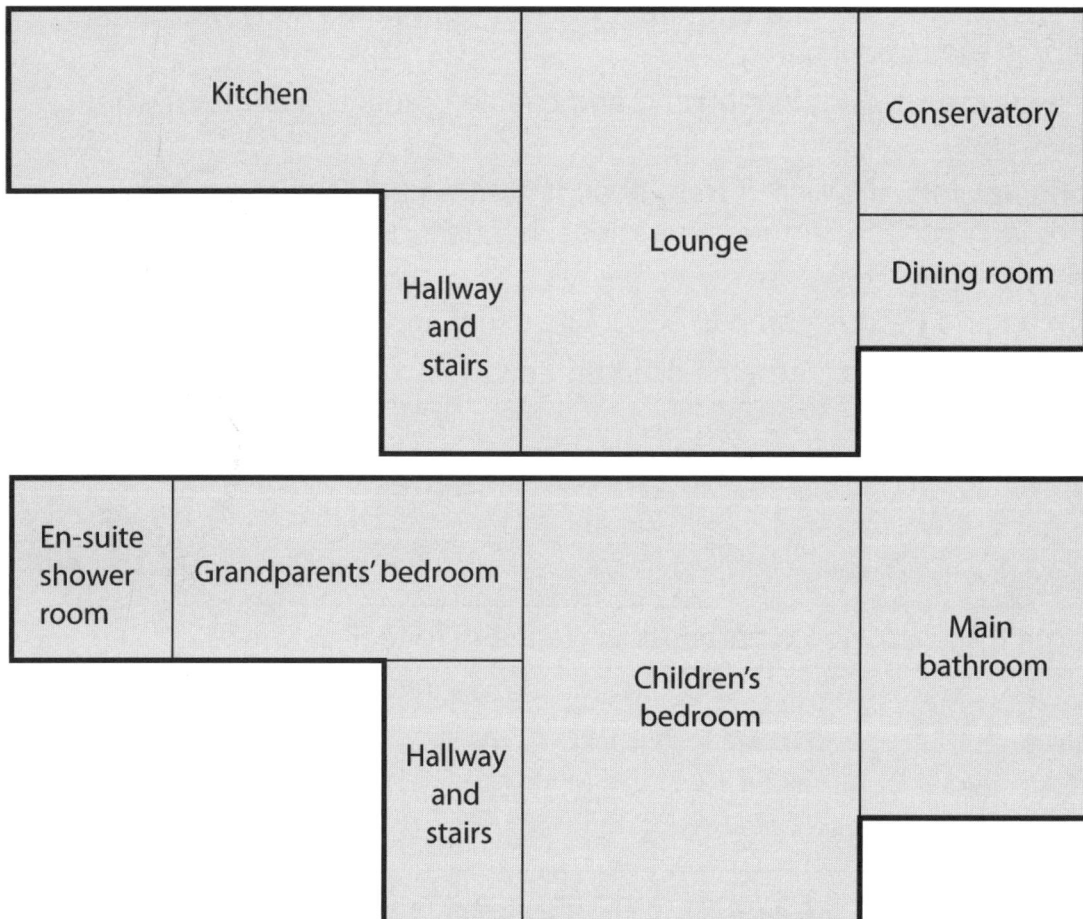

Kitchen		Conservatory
	Lounge	Dining room
Hallway and stairs		

En-suite shower room	Grandparents' bedroom		Main bathroom
	Hallway and stairs	Children's bedroom	

2. Write a shopping list of safety items needed to help make the house safer.

CFC3
AC 3.1, 3.2
CFC24
AC 2.1, 2.2

4.A7 Garden safety

1. Matthew and Alan's grandfather is worried about the safety of the garden. Can you identify seven potential hazards in the picture?

2. Grandfather is very good at DIY and woodwork. What can he do to make the garden safer?

4.A8 Grandfather's toys

Matthew and Alan's grandfather has found some toys for when they come to stay for the weekend. Grandmother is not sure they are safe for the boys to play with. Matthew is 3 years old and Alan is 1 year old.

1. Grandfather has bought some board games from a car boot sale. All the pieces are there even though they are not in the box. Why might these be unsafe?

2. Grandfather also cleared out the attic and found some toys that used to belong to Matthew and Alan's father when he was little. He has cleaned them all up so they are no longer dusty. Why might these toys be unsuitable for the children?

3. The lady who lives next door makes teddy bears in her spare time. She has given Grandfather one for each of the children. Would these toys be safe for the children? Why/why not?

4.A9 Cleaning around the house

Read through each scenario and identify the potential hazard.

1. Karen accidently splits the packet when she opens some toilet cleaning wipes. To prevent them from drying out she places them inside a baby wipes box.

Danger
What might happen?

2. Funmi has spilt some bleach on the bathroom floor, but she is running late and does not have time to wipe it up.

Danger
What might happen?

3. Ollie uses bleach to clean his trainers and keep them sparkly white. He has found that using a toothbrush is ideal to get in the creases. He rinses the toothbrush and leaves it to soak in water so he can use it later.

Danger
What might happen?

4.A10 Taking Tom and Ellis out

Taking small children out of the house – even for a short trip – needs to be planned before you leave.

Tom and Ellis want to go to the local park to play in the playground after school. It is five minutes away and you will need to cross two roads on the way.

1. Explain some rules and responsibilities you have and that the children have themselves when going to the park. You should also think about what safety measures you should take. Jot some notes in the boxes below.

You	Find a zebra crossing
Tom and Ellis	Hold hands when crossing the road

2. When you arrive at the park you find the playground has:

- a dog off its lead
- a broken glass bottle on the ground
- damage to the swings.

Suggest some sensible advice or actions you might take to make the park safer for the children to play in.

3. Tom and Ellis's mum will pick you up from the park in her car. How can you and the children travel safely in the car and why is this important?

4.A11 Fire safety

Thinking about fire safety is important because in the case of a real fire, there is no time to be indecisive.

1. There is a range of items available to help alert us to or put out fires should they start. Read the list and explain what their use might be and what might prevent their effective use.

Item	Its use	What might prevent its effective use?
Smoke alarm		
Fire extinguisher		
Fire blanket		

2. There are some items that increase the risk of a house fire. Look at each item and suggest how to minimise the risk of fire.

Candles	
Chip pans	
Cigarettes	
Damaged wire on electrical items	
Tea towels next to the cooker	

3. Consider an escape plan in the event of a fire in your own house. Write your plan down. Remember you should never try to tackle the fire yourself, so you need to think about escaping as quickly and safely as possible.

4.H1 Safety guidance and labelling

Children's toys need to be safe for them to play with. They also need to be safe even if the child does not play with them properly or if they take them apart.

Safety symbols

In order to make sure that toys are safe for children, there are symbols and labels parents and carers can look out for when buying toys.

The CE mark identifies that the item is intended to be a toy and it should be safe. CE stands for European Community. The CE mark could be on a label or box that the toy came in.

This is a Lion Mark. It is good to see on a toy. It means it has been made by a member of the British Toy and Hobby Association. Their members make safe and quality toys.

Regulations

The law which states that toys must be safe for children to play with is the Toy Safety Regulations (1995). Trading Standards make sure that toys are suitable for children and will investigate and may prosecute companies if toys are unsafe.

Age guidance

You can also look out for age guides on toys that will tell you whether it is unsafe for children under a certain age to play with some toys. This might be because they contain small pieces which children could put into their mouths, or because they could hurt young children in some other way.

Most of this information is contained on the box the toy came in or in its instructions, so it is important to keep both for future reference.

It is also important to remember that old toys are not likely to have passed the safety tests we use today and so they might not be safe for use. They could also have become damaged or broken over time.

4.H2 Symbols on household products

Some commonly used household cleaning materials can be dangerous if they are not stored and used correctly.

It is important to read instructions carefully and always follow the manufacturer's guidance.

Below are some symbols you might find on household products.

Flammable – this means that you need to keep the product away from fire and heat sources.

Toxic – this product is toxic if swallowed, inhaled or if it comes into contact with skin.

Harmful – this product is harmful if swallowed, inhaled or if it comes into contact with skin.

Corrosive – this product will cause damage if it comes into contact with skin.

Dangerous to the environment

Any product containing these labels must be handled with extreme care.

There are some general rules about using cleaning products to ensure safety:

- Clean up any spills straight away.
- Always follow the instructions for use.
- Replace the cap immediately and discard a product if the cap is broken.
- Store all products safely out of the reach of children in a locked cupboard.
- Wash off any splashes immediately.
- Never refill bottles or containers with another product.

Introduction

This chapter covers:

E3 CFC4 Routines for a young child

Routine creates balance in a child's life. A daily routine which includes regular mealtimes, bath time and bedtime provides a young child with a sense of security and helps them to develop good personal and healthy eating habits. It should also ensure that they take enough exercise and rest.

This chapter will give learners an understanding of the importance of a daily routine for young children aged 1 to 2 years old. They will learn how different activities structure a child's day. Learners will find out what a healthy diet for a 2 year old is and what clothes and protection should be given to children in different weather. They will also need to understand the requirements of a sleeping area and how different activities prepare a young child for bedtime.

Learning outcomes

Unit CFC4 has four learning outcomes:

1. Understand the role of a routine in the care of a young child.
2. Know about the need for a healthy diet for the young child.
3. Know how to dress a young child for different weather.
4. Know how to support a young child to restful sleep.

Teacher checklist

✓ Understand the benefits of a daily routine for a young child

✓ Describe a healthy diet for a young child

✓ Understand how to clothe a young child for different types of weather

✓ Describe an appropriate sleeping area for a young child

✓ Appreciate a child's need for a calming routine at the end of each day

---

There are links between this unit and units CFC7 Eating healthily, CFC20 Healthy eating for families and HL1 Healthy living. After looking at routines and healthy eating for young children, learners can reflect on their own diets and lifestyles and how healthy they are.

Additional guidance for delivery

Lessons on daily routines for children can be extended by asking learners to look at their own daily routines. A discussion centring on what learners could do to have a healthier lifestyle can be useful.

A number of active or practical sessions can be used to reinforce the material in this chapter. Suggestions include using food magazines and cookery books to enhance sessions on healthy diets for young children, perhaps even extending this to include cookery; asking groups of students to produce posters illustrating suitable clothing for children or a suitable sleeping area using images from clothing and DIY catalogues and paint swatches.

Inviting someone in to demonstrate how they bath their baby would enrich the learners' experience, but if this is not possible, and if suitable practical room is available, you could provide dolls and baby baths for a practical session.

As a group, or on an individual basis, ask the learners to complete the interactive **Knowledge check** to finish the chapter.

Further resources

Ann Tapp (2008) *CACHE Entry Level Certificate: Preparation for child care*, Pearson Education Ltd

www.mothercare.co.uk

www.pre-school.org.uk

Various NHS web pages including:

www.nhs.uk/Planners/birthtofive/Pages/Babyessentialshub.aspx

www.nhs.uk/Planners/birthtofive/Pages/Healthydietweaninghub.aspx

Answers to activities

5.A4

1. proof/retardant/resistant; 2. hat, warm, sun; 3. buttons; 4. velcro; 5. nylon; 6. cotton; 7. weather; 8. big/large/baggy/loose; 9. small/tight; 10. blisters, deformed; 11. up, down; 12. measured, shoes, growing/developing

5.A7

1. Undress the baby…; 2. Reassure the baby…; 3. Wrap the baby in a warm towel and wash his face; 4. Hold baby over the bath and wash baby's hair; 5. Lower baby feet first…; 6. With your free hand…; 7. Take baby out of the bath…; 8. Put on a clean nappy…

5.A9

1. storybook; 2. milky drink; 3. teddy; 4. talking time; 5. rhyme; 6. light; 7. hug; 8. bath; 9. kiss goodnight

Q	S	O	C	A	H	G	U	O	M	Y	T	L	P	E
D	T	A	L	K	I	N	G	T	I	M	E	O	U	S
R	O	T	O	R	Y	T	I	M	L	T	D	O	T	I
E	R	H	Y	M	E	S	P	L	K	T	D	P	N	A
S	Y	H	S	E	N	D	R	O	Y	A	Y	L	E	R
S	B	E	C	O	N	F	I	D	D	N	C	E	M	P
I	O	L	I	A	L	O	S	A	R	M	H	N	B	G
N	O	I	N	T	I	B	E	C	I	A	U	M	A	O
G	K	I	S	S	G	O	O	D	N	I	G	H	T	P
U	Z	S	A	O	H	M	C	I	K	P	E	H	H	O
P	A	I	N	T	T	N	G	E	T	E	R	L	U	A

Chapter 5 Care of children

Overview of resources

Resources	Teaching notes	Link to Student Book	Link to Units and assessment criteria
5.A1 The needs of a child	This activity encourages learners to think about the basic needs of children. Learners should work in small groups to brainstorm examples of each basic need. Learners can then write a sentence using their examples to show an understanding of each need. Whole class feedback can be used to add more examples.		**CFC4** *AC 1.1*
5.H1 The benefits of a routine	This handout illustrates how routine in a child's life is beneficial in their overall development and gives examples of behaviour which might develop if there is a lack of routine. To use this as an activity before giving out the handout the points can be printed off and attached to 'Jenga' blocks, learners can then draw a block and discuss each of the points before returning it to the top of the pile.	p.86–87	**CFC4** *AC 1.1, 1.2*
5.A2 Daily routine	This activity encourages learners to think about suitable activities for a 2 year old and to put them into a daily routine. Learners should be encouraged to consider the timing of each activity and to note this in the correct column. An extension to this activity could be to find out what facilities are available in the learners' local area and make a daily or weekly plan around these.	p.87	**CFC4** *AC 1.1*
5.A3 Healthy diet	To introduce this activity it would be useful to recap material from Chapter 3 Healthy living, Student Book, pages 44–63. Learners can use children's menu books, magazines or the Internet to plan a healthy selection of meals and snacks. An extension of this activity: using paper plates and pictures learners create a healthy eating display. It may also be useful to bring in suitable foods as examples to learners.	p.88–89	**CFC4** *AC 2.1*
5.A4 Children's clothing	Depending on each learner's ability you may want to give out the missing words for this gap fill activity. Each point can be used for discussion work, e.g. suitable fastenings or encouraging independence when potty training.	p.90–91	**CFC4** *AC 3.1*
5.A5 Clothes for all weather	Learners should make a list of the clothing required for each type of weather. Using the list the learner should explain why they have chosen each item of clothing. An extension of this would be for learners to explain what would happen if the child was not wearing the proper clothing to protect them from the weather, and why it is important that clothing fits properly.	p.90–91	**CFC4** *AC 3.1*

Resources	Teaching notes	Link to Student Book	Link to Units and assessment criteria
5.A6 Sleeping areas	This activity sheet includes a bedroom plan and a shopping list and you may or may not include a budget for your learners. Learners plan a bedroom suitable for a 2 year old. They will need to consider: heating, lighting, wall and floor coverings, furniture and storage, soft furnishings. Learners can use paint charts, wallpaper swatches and material samples for inspiration, as well as catalogues. They will need to pay careful attention to health and safety. For an extension activity learners could provide written information explaining their reasons for certain choices; there could also be discussion work around this. Learners may produce larger bedroom plans for display purposes, e.g. on A3 paper.	p.92	**CFC4** *AC 4.1*
5.A7 Bathing a baby	This activity sheet would support a practical session. Learners consider the steps of preparing and bathing a baby. Learners order the steps for bathing a baby; this can be done after an observation in the classroom using a bath and baby doll. Some learners may find it easier if the points are cut into strips that can be moved around and then stuck down in the correct order once they have been checked. As an extension, learners work in small groups to suggest ways in which good hygiene habits for hair, teeth, bathing, clothing and hands can be encouraged, e.g. with the use of bath toys, 'fun' toothbrushes, etc.		**CFC4** *AC 4.2*
5.A8 Bedtime routine	Learners can work in small groups or pairs to discuss the order of the activities. They should cut and paste the words onto a sheet in the correct order and then add a suitable time. Answers to this may vary and learners should be able to give reasons for their choices when questioned. An extension to this activity would be for learners to write up an explanation of their answers.	p.93	**CFC4** *AC 4.2*
5.A9 Calming activities	Learners complete the word search by answering the questions and then finding the answers on the grid. This can be tackled as an individual activity, or by putting the learners into groups to solve the questions before they attempt the word search. The tutor may provide the answers to the questions at the beginning of the activity if they feel it necessary.	p.93	**CFC4** *AC 4.2*
Electronic resources			
5.PPT Caring for children	This PowerPoint presentation explores aspects of caring for children in a way that meets their needs and rights (including those set out in law). The importance of routine that is age and stage appropriate is also covered.		
Knowledge Check	Interactive quiz covering learning from the units in the chapter for consideration purposes. You could run the quiz via the VLE with learners during the first session to see how much they already know; it could be done again later to see how much progress they have made. Alternatively, more independent learners could have a go at completing the quiz on their own.		

5.A1 The needs of a child

A basic need is something that we cannot live without. Think about the needs of a child aged 1 to 2.

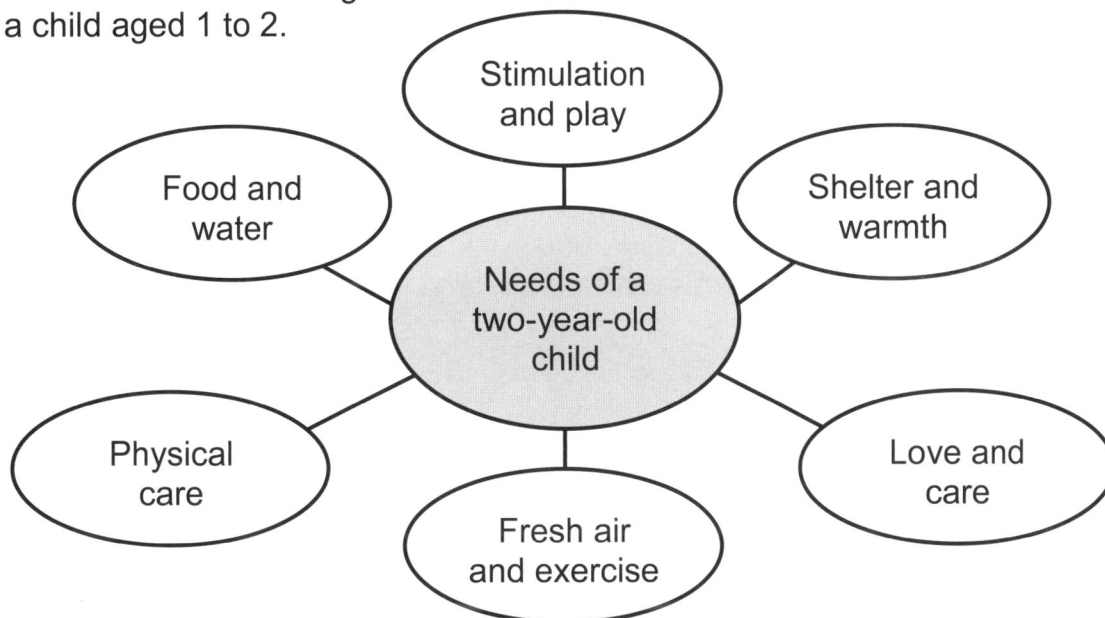

```
        ┌─────────────┐
        │ Stimulation │
        │  and play   │
        └─────────────┘
┌──────────┐         ┌──────────┐
│ Food and │         │Shelter and│
│  water   │         │  warmth  │
└──────────┘         └──────────┘
        ┌─────────────┐
        │  Needs of a │
        │ two-year-old│
        │    child    │
        └─────────────┘
┌──────────┐         ┌──────────┐
│ Physical │         │ Love and │
│   care   │         │   care   │
└──────────┘         └──────────┘
        ┌─────────────┐
        │  Fresh air  │
        │ and exercise│
        └─────────────┘
```

Think about each of the basic needs that a small child aged between 1 and 2 has. Can you give three examples of each basic need? An example has been done already.

Shelter and warmth
- *Housing*
-
-

Fresh air and exercise
-
-
-

Food and water
-
-
-

Love and care
-
-
-

Physical care
-
-
-

Stimulation and play
-
-
-

Can you write a sentence using your examples of each of these to show an understanding of each of the basic needs? Use a separate piece of paper to do this.

5.A2 Daily routine

You are looking after a 2 year old for 24 hours. Using the timeline below, plan out a full day from getting up until going to bed.

Write the name of each activity. Write the time you want each activity to happen. The first and last activity have been given already but you need to write down what time you want them to happen.

Here are some activities for you to choose from: dressing, singing, hygiene, snack time, toddler group, walk to the park, nap time, story time, lunch time, tea time, breakfast time, quiet time, play time, bath time.

	Time	Activity
		Getting up
		Bedtime

5.A3 Healthy diet

You need to make a diet plan for one day for a 2 year old. Write your ideas for meals, snacks and drinks in the table below.

Remember that it should be a balanced diet and contain: carbohydrates, fruit and vegetables (at least five portions a day), dairy (at least three portions a day), protein and a small amount of fat and sugar.

Breakfast	Food: Drink:			
Snack				
Lunch	Food: Drink:			
Snack				
Tea	Food: Drink:			
Other drinks				

Food and drink ideas:

milk	cereal	fruit juice
popcorn	yoghurt	mince
vegetable sticks	grapes	rice
eggs	potatoes	water
houmous	cheese	pasta
wholemeal bread	dried fruit	beans
banana	vegetables	salad

5.A4 Children's clothing

How much do you know about children's clothing?
Look at the sentences below and fill in the gaps.

1. Clothes need to be flame _____ to keep children safe from fire.

2. A child needs a _____ in winter to keep their head _____ and in the summer to protect the child's head from the _____.

3. Children struggle to get _____ into holes, especially if they are small.

4. Shoes fastened with _____ help children to put their own shoes on and encourage independence.

5. _____ is not a good material to use for children's clothing; it does not allow the skin to breathe and the child will get hot and uncomfortable.

6. _____ is a material that lets skin breathe and is best for allergies; it is best to choose clothing made from this.

7. Clothes must be suitable for the _____, in winter and summer.

8. If clothes are too _____ they may fall down, or the child may trip over.

9. If clothes are too _____ they will cut into the skin and cause discomfort to the child.

10. Shoes that are the wrong size cause _____ or _____ toes.

11. When a child is being potty trained clothes should be easy to pull _____ and _____.

12. Children grow very quickly. You should have their feet _____ regularly so that they are not wearing shoes that are too tight. If a child's _____ are too small they can stop the feet _____ properly.

5.A5 Clothes for all weather

You need to dress a child aged 1 to 2 years old. They will be outside in very different types of weather.

You need to consider the following: protection from the weather, underwear, footwear, safety, materials that the clothing is made from and practicality, e.g. washing.

1. Make a list of clothing for each type of weather.

A hot sunny day	A rainy day
List of clothes	List of clothes
•	•
•	•
•	•
•	•
•	•
•	•
•	•
•	•
•	•

A bitterly cold day	A windy day
List of clothes	List of clothes
•	•
•	•
•	•
•	•
•	•
•	•
•	•
•	•

2. On a separate sheet explain why you have chosen each item of clothing.

3. Explain what might happen if the child was not wearing the proper clothing to protect them from the weather and why it is important that the clothing fits properly.

5.A6 Sleeping areas

In the space below, plan a bedroom for a 2 year old.

Include at least one window and a door. Think about heating and lighting, wall and floor coverings, as well as the furniture you will need for storage and sleeping. You will need to consider soft furnishings such as rugs, bedding, curtains and lampshades.

Use magazines and the Internet to cost out all of your items and write them in the shopping list. You may have to keep to a budget so keep an eye on how much you spend.

Don't forget health and safety in your planning.

You could stick samples of paint, wallpaper, fabrics and flooring you think are suitable to a separate piece of paper.

Bedroom plan	Shopping list	
	Item	**Cost**

5.A7 Bathing a baby

When bathing a baby, start by getting everything that you need ready including:

- a towel
- toiletries such as a baby soap or liquid wash (soap is not necessary for newborn babies)
- a clean nappy
- clothes.

Make sure that the room is at a comfortable temperature. Fill the bath with about 5 cm of warm water. Test the water temperature with your wrist or elbow – it should be 36°C and not feel hot.

Never leave a baby alone in the water, even for a second. If you have to go somewhere, wrap the baby in a towel and take him or her with you.

Bathing can become part of a bedtime routine; it will help mark the change from daytime to bedtime.

Can you order the steps of bathing a baby? Put numbers in the boxes to put the following steps in the correct order.

Step number	
	Hold baby over the bath and wash baby's hair
	With your free hand, gently splash water over baby's body
	Take baby out of the bath and wrap him in a warm towel and pat him dry
	Undress the baby and clean the nappy area
	Reassure baby by chatting to him – this will help him to feel safe
	Wrap the baby in a warm towel and wash his face
	Lower baby feet first into the water – remember to support his head and neck at all times
	Put on a clean nappy and dress baby

5.A8 Bedtime routine

Cut out the boxes below and paste them onto a piece of paper in the correct order.

Write the time below each one to show what time you think it should happen.

(Remember that parents have their own routines for children so this is a personal order.)

Clean teeth	Lights out
Milky drink	Door closed
Toilet	Bedtime story
Bath time	Hug and kiss goodnight

5.A9 Calming activities

Answer these questions and then find the words in the grid below.

1. Something you could read to a child, nothing too long or too scary
2. Something warm and full of goodness that you put in a cup
3. A soft toy to cuddle, they like to picnic in the woods!
4. Take this to chat about your day together
5. Sing these with the child
6. You may need to switch this on at night if children are frightened of the dark
7. You need your arms for this
8. A calming activity that can be part of the child's hygiene routine
9. The last thing you do to settle the child.

Q	S	O	C	A	H	G	U	O	M	Y	T	L	P	E
D	T	A	L	K	I	N	G	T	I	M	E	O	U	S
R	O	T	O	R	Y	T	I	M	L	T	D	O	T	I
E	R	H	Y	M	E	S	P	L	K	T	D	P	N	A
S	Y	H	S	E	N	D	R	O	Y	A	Y	L	E	R
S	B	E	C	O	N	F	I	D	D	N	C	E	M	P
I	O	L	I	A	L	O	S	A	R	M	H	N	B	G
N	O	I	N	T	I	B	E	C	I	A	U	M	A	O
G	K	I	S	S	G	O	O	D	N	I	G	H	T	P
U	Z	S	A	O	H	M	C	I	K	P	E	H	H	O
P	A	I	N	T	T	N	G	E	T	E	R	L	U	A

5.H1 The benefits of a routine

Positive effects of a routine

A routine helps a child to develop. Rules and boundaries, set meal times, rest times and bedtimes have lots of benefits to a child. A routine makes a child sure of what is allowed and what is good and healthy.

Some of the benefits of a routine include:

- good attitude with people
- confidence to try new things
- high self-esteem
- confidence in abilities
- rested
- good concentration skills
- good appetite
- manners
- develop good habits
- feel secure.

Negative effects of no routine

A child with no routine may learn bad habits and unhealthy behaviour. The child will be unsure of what is allowed and what is right and wrong. This is bad for a young child.

A young child with no routine might:

- develop poor social skills
- have tantrums
- feel insecure
- lack concentration
- be tired
- have a poor appetite
- display inappropriate behaviour.

Introduction

This chapter covers:

E3 CFC2 Listening to and talking with a young child

L1 CFC9 Respecting and valuing children

Acknowledging children's rights as individuals requires those who work with them to communicate effectively.

Learners will begin to understand what affects language both negatively and positively and how they can use activities to promote speaking and listening with young children. By demonstrating active listening children will feel valued and respected.

Importance is also placed upon communication with pre-verbal babies, as inexperienced practitioners might fail to see the value in talking to young babies who cannot verbally respond.

Participation is essential in upholding children's rights and demonstrating that they are valued. This is a right enshrined within the United Nations Convention on the Rights of the Child (1989) and so learners should be encouraged to think about whether in reality children are active participants in their learning and care environments.

Learners will gain understanding of how participatory methods can be used with young children by experiencing these for themselves in Activity 6.A8.

Learning outcomes

Unit CFC2

Unit CFC2 has two learning outcomes:

1. Know skills for communicating with a young child.
2. Understand activities that will develop a child's talking and listening skills.

Teacher checklist
✓ What demonstrates active listening
✓ The importance of communication with pre-verbal babies
✓ How to communicate with pre-verbal babies
✓ Why reading stories promotes good communication
✓ How to engage children in story time sessions

Unit CFC9

Unit CFC9 has three learning outcomes:

1. Know how to respect and value children as individuals.
2. Understand ways to respect and value children.
3. Know that children have rights.

Teacher checklist
✓ Ways of respecting and valuing children by listening to them
✓ The ways that children can participate within their environments
✓ How to promote self-esteem and confidence in children
✓ What rights children have
✓ Which agencies help to uphold these rights for children

Learners will notice some strong links between Unit CFC9 Respecting and valuing children and Unit IRRE3 Individual rights and responsibilities.

Additional guidance for delivery

Activity 6.A3 provides learners with an opportunity to develop the theme of storytelling. This could form part of a more in-depth study including the opportunity to make displays, take part in craft activities and consider the value of storytelling to young children.

In order for learners to understand how to value others it is important that they feel valued and respected themselves. Activity 6.A5 should be handled carefully. Learners might want to consider areas that are sensitive such as weight. By undertaking this activity learners will understand how being placed within one group fails to allow them to be seen in their entirety – thus they will understand the concept of discrimination and stereotyping.

The 'rosy glow' activity in 6.A6 should reinforce positive self-image and self-esteem by receiving peer recognition for their attributes and positive characteristics.

Activity 6.A9 requires learners to undertake research so use of library resources would be helpful for this purpose.

As a group, or on an individual basis, ask the learners to complete the interactive **Knowledge check** to finish the chapter.

Further resources

Department for Children Schools and Families (2008), *Every Child a Talker: Guidance for Early Language Lead Professionals*, DCSF Publications, Nottingham

www.bookstart.org.uk

Recommendations for books to read with babies and young children and resources including activities for children and families.

www.literacytrust.org.uk/talk_to_your_baby

This website provides up to date research and policy, resources and advice for developing literacy and communication with babies and children.

www.rights4me.org

This website speaks directly to children about what rights they have and how they can exercise these if they are living away from home, for example in boarding school.

http://www.unicef.org/rightsite/files/uncrcchilldfriendlylanguage.pdf

A child-friendly, downloadable poster of the United Nations Convention on the Rights of the Child (1989) Articles.

Chapter 6 Communicating with children

Overview of resources

Resources	Teaching notes	Link to Student Book	Link to Units and assessment criteria
6.A1 Listen to me	Listening is an essential part of communication. Learners need to understand the importance of listening and responding in a way that demonstrates they are listening. This activity should be completed in pairs or small groups. You could follow up this activity by playing 'Chinese whispers' with the group, starting with a simple sentence and finishing with a complex one.	p.98–99 p.106	**CFC2** AC 1.1, 1.2 **CFC9** AC 2.1
6.A2 Babbling baby	It is important to listen and respond to non-verbal babies. This activity encourages learners to think about negative and positive influences upon early speaking. Learners also need to think about activities that might promote language such as peek-a-boo, songs and rhymes and reading stories to babies.	p.98–99 p.106	**CFC2** AC 1.1, 1.2 **CFC9** AC 2.1
6.H1 Billy goat's coats **6.A3** Sizzling story time	Story time is an important activity to help children to listen and respond. Activity 6.H1 is a short story for young children. Learners will read through the story and create activities linked to the story and its characters. Activity 6.A3 encourages learners to develop ideas for storytelling and making stories come alive for young children. This is a creative and craft-based activity that requires learners to work in groups. It also makes suggestions for displays that could be planned or made.	p.100	**CFC2** AC 2.1, 2.2, 2.3
6.A4 I am unique	This activity reinforces that we all have similarities, but are individual. Learners will gain an understanding of what it means to be part of a group and have similarities yet remain an individual.		**CFC9** AC 1.1, 1.2
6.A5 I belong	Building upon Activity 6.A4, learners will explore their individuality and needs. Sensitivity needs to be exercised in this activity where learners consider groups or features they would rather not be part of. An example might be where a learner is a smoker.	p.104–7	**CFC9** AC 1.1, 1.2
6.A6 The rosy little glow	This activity promotes self-esteem and confidence, an important starting point for learners to consider how they can value and respect others. Learners write their names at the top of their sheet and pass it to their left. Every learner writes a positive comment about the person in the box and then passes it on to the next person. At the end, each learner will have a set of positive comments about themselves.	p.104–7	**CFC9** AC 2.2

Resources	Teaching notes	Link to Student Book	Link to Units and assessment criteria
6.A7 Feeling different	Learners will examine the case studies and suggest how each child can be helped to feel valued and respected. The action plan should suggest ways of helping the child to feel more included in their setting. Learners will also reflect upon how the child feels at the moment, and how the action plan might make them feel.	p.104–105	**CFC9** AC 2.2
6.A8 The class council	Respecting and valuing children can be best achieved through active participation. This is enshrined in the United Nations Convention on the Rights of the Child (1989), Article 12. Activity 6.A8 encourages learners to think about participation through school councils. This activity is a lively small group and whole class activity that requires learners to vote for a class spokesperson.	p.106–7	**CFC9** AC 2.1, 2.2
6.A9 Researching organisations	Learners are to explore the organisations that are in place to help to promote the rights of children. Activity 6.A9 provides them with a framework to undertake research and to develop a fact sheet designed to help children understand how the organisation could benefit them.	p.106–7	**CFC9** AC 3.1
Electronic resources			
6.PPT Communicating with children	This PowerPoint presentation provides a brief overview of 'active listening', the importance of story time for young children and summarises how individuality and belonging need to be supported in children. This will introduce the learners to the key topics they will cover in this chapter.		
Knowledge Check	Interactive quiz covering learning from the units in the chapter for consolidation purposes. You could run the quiz via the VLE with learners during the first session to see how much they already know; it could be done again later to see how much progress they have made. Alternatively, more independent learners could have a go at completing the quiz on their own.		

6.A1 Listen to me

These activities need to be completed in pairs or small groups.

It is important to demonstrate to children that you are listening to them and valuing what they say.

1. Imagine that you are responding to a child. Using only body language, show that you are:

   - scared
   - shocked
   - pleased
   - excited.

2. Now imagine that you are working with young children. Demonstrating that you are interested and value what they are saying, respond verbally to the following:

   - Look! I am a lion, grrrrrrr…
   - There is a crocodile in the toilet.
   - I have done my buttons up all by myself.
   - It is my birthday tomorrow.

3. It is important that you give children the chance to talk, even if they cannot use full sentences.

   Circle the actions below that would show you are valuing the child when listening to them.

Smile	Finish their sentence for them
Nod	Make eye contact
Carry on with what you are doing	Turn away
Say 'Shhh'	Bend over them
Yawn	Bend down to their level
Ask questions	

4. Now role play the answers you have given to question 3, and discuss how it feels with your partner.

6.A2 Babbling baby

Read the information about each child below.

> Perry is 6 months old. He blows raspberries, coos and babbles.
>
> Perry has three sisters and loves playing with them.
>
> His parents sing nursery rhymes to him and ask him questions and pretend that he answers.

> Louise is 7 months old. She does not make many sounds.
>
> Louise has her dummy most of the time unless she is drinking from her bottle.
>
> She sits on the floor watching television most of the day.
>
> Louise's parents do not speak to her much because they think she is too little.

1. What things do you think have helped Perry to start to practise talking?

2. What might help Louise to begin to practise talking?

3. What activities could you play with both babies to help them to develop their speech further?

6.A3 Sizzling story time

Stories are important for young children.

Now you have read through the story *Billy goat's coats*, complete the following activities.

1. Make the story come alive by creating some characters for the story. Then use your characters to retell the story to your group. You could:
   - draw pictures
   - make puppets
   - use photographs
   - make models.

2. Now imagine that you are going to read *Billy goat's coats* to a group of young children. What props might you let the children play with or look at while you tell the story?

3. Children like repetition and rhymes. Can you think up another story or rhyme using Billy goat?

4. Design a display that children can interact with around the story *Billy goat's coats*. You might want to make it 3D or include items the children can play with.

The College of West Anglia
Learning Resource Centre

6.A4 I am unique

In this activity you will consider yourself and someone else in your group who you know.

1. List all the things you have in common and all the things that are different. An example has been completed for you.

The same	Different
Both 17 years old	Does not wear glasses

2. Do you have more things in common than are different?

3. Consider three things that make you individual and different from everyone else in your group. Write them in the stars below.

6.A5 I belong

You are an individual but you might belong to various groups or be identified by other features.

1. Try to think of as many different ways in which you are identified as you can. A few suggestions have been done for you.

> I am…
> *female/male*
> *a student*
> *a member of the gym*

2. Are there any groups or features that you would rather not be identified by?

3. Do you need to attend any special places or have any special equipment in order to be you? For example, *I am short sighted – I need to wear glasses.*

6.A6 The rosy little glow

Write your name at the top and then pass this piece of paper to your left. Make sure that every person makes a POSITIVE comment on every other person's sheet in the group. An example has been written in the first line.

Name..

I like the way you share your sweets with everyone.

6.A7 Feeling different

Read through each scenario below and suggest an action plan to help the child feel respected and valued.

1. Gareth is the only child in his class with a Welsh accent; even his teacher keeps saying, 'Pardon?' when he speaks. Now he does not want to talk any more.

How Gareth feels now　　　Action plan　　　How it will make Gareth feel

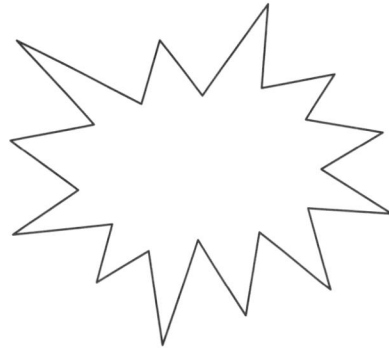

2. Jack has restricted growth in one arm. He always wears long-sleeved T-shirts and feels different from everyone else at nursery. How can he be helped to feel more included?

How Jack feels now　　　Action plan　　　How it will make Jack feel

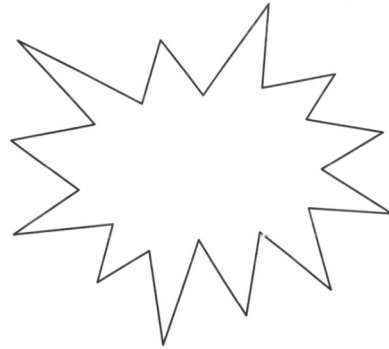

3. It is Eid, a special occasion for Khaleeda. She feels disappointed that no one else at her school even knows what this is.

How Khaleeda feels now　　　Action plan　　　How it will make Khaleeda feel

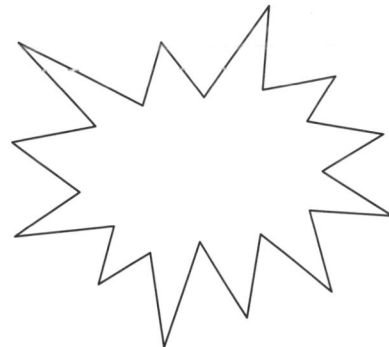

6.A8 The class council

One of the best ways to help children to feel valued, respected and to make sure that their voices are heard is to allow them to participate in things that involve them.

Even the law says that this is a good idea. (The United Nations Convention on the Rights of the Child (1989), Article 12).

1. In small groups choose a person to stand as class spokesperson.

   The group is the campaign team, so you need to work together to make an election presentation, which should last about 2 minutes.

   Your group needs to convince the rest of the class that your candidate will be the best person to speak for them and help to uphold their rights if elected. The class will then vote for their favourite candidate.

   Fill in the table below:

Why your candidate should be elected	What will they do to benefit the class?

2. As a small group, think about a realistic change you would like to make within your class.

   You will need to consider why this will benefit every member of your class. You will then make a proposal to your newly elected class spokesperson to persuade them to make the change happen.

   As a group vote upon what change you want.

Some pointers:

- *Your change should be practical – more break and less lesson time will see you fail your course!*

- *It should not break rules; these have been devised to make your learning environment safe and effective.*

6.A9 Researching organisations

1. You are going to research organisations that promote the rights of children. Choose one organisation.

Possible places to start your research are:
- NSPCC
- Save the Children
- Children's Rights Alliance for England
- UNICEF
- Action for Children

You can use this table to help you organise your research.

What is the name of the organisation and how can you contact them?	Write **two** things that the organisation does to help children.	Does the organisation have any current campaigns?	Find out **two** more pieces of information about the organisation.

2. Now you know what the chosen organisation does, plan a fact sheet for children who might need to contact the organisation.

   Your fact sheet could include ways in which the child can contact the organisation and what support they can offer.

6.H1 Billy goat's coats

In a field, on a farm, lived a little goat called Billy.

'Brrrrr, I am cold, I need a new coat', said Billy.

So off he trotted to find himself a new coat.

First he stopped at a busy road. In the middle of the road was a lollipop lady. She was wearing a bright yellow coat.

Billy tried it on…

'Oh no Billy, don't be silly, that coat isn't right for a goat', said the lollipop lady.

Next Billy went into a fire station. The firefighters were wearing big heavy coats to protect them.

Billy tried one on…

'Oh no Billy, don't be silly, that coat isn't right for a goat', said the firefighter.

Finally Billy sneaked into the doctor's surgery and saw the doctor's white coat.

Billy tried it on…

'Oh no Billy, don't be silly, that coat isn't right for a goat', said the doctor.

Billy trotted sadly back to the farm. Then he saw the farmer.

The farmer had made a special coat for Billy, not too bright, nor too heavy, nor too white.

It was a coat for a goat and it was just right.

Introduction

This chapter covers:

E3 CFC1 Confidence building for the young child through play

E3 CFC5 Play and learning in the home

L1 CFC13 Sharing learning experiences with children

L1 CFC17 Supporting babies to play

L1 Understanding play for early learning

This is a large chapter which explores the importance of play and how, through the correct kinds of play, learning can take place. It looks at different activities which can help with all areas of development. Health and safety is included too.

The role of the adult in providing for play is considered along with positive ways an adult can support children's play to encourage independence. A visit to a local day nursery is an excellent start to this chapter as some learners have little idea of how children in a nursery play and learn.

Learning outcomes

Unit CFC1

Unit CFC1 has two learning outcomes:

1. Know the support a young child needs to gain confidence through play.
2. Know how to encourage a young child to express their feelings through play.

Teacher checklist
✓   Look at the importance of using positive language when talking to children about their work
✓   Plan activities which support children's emotional development
✓   How adult interaction supports the child's self-esteem
✓   The importance of toys and activities that are age/stage appropriate

Unit CFC5

Unit CFC5 has two learning outcomes:

1. Know ways to provide play in the home for a young child.
2. Understand the role of the adult during play in the home.

Teacher checklist
✓   Look at how children can learn through playing with everyday items in the home
✓   How an adult can support and extend play in the home
✓   How the adult needs to think about safety and support the child through play
✓   The introduction of a treasure basket to young children to support sensory development

Unit CFC13

Unit CFC13 has four learning outcomes:

1. Know how children learn.
2. Know how to use stories and rhymes with young children.
3. Understand that the natural world can support children's learning.
4. Know how the local community can be used to broaden children's experiences.

Teacher checklist

- ✓ Examples of songs and rhymes to encourage language development (works well with learners if you use instruments so they have 'something to hide behind')
- ✓ Learners need to have suitable stories so they can have a go at reading stories to each other
- ✓ The use of different story sacks for a practical session
- ✓ Visiting local library if possible for a story telling session

Unit CFC17

Unit CFC1 has three learning outcomes:

1. Know how babies' development is supported by play.
2. Know about play activities for babies.
3. Know the role of the adult in providing play for babies.

Teacher checklist

- ✓ How play supports children's all round development
- ✓ Making sure children's toys are suitable/age and stage appropriate
- ✓ Why it is important for babies to play

Unit Understanding play for early learning

Unit Understanding play for early learning has three learning outcomes:

1. Understand the features of a positive learning environment.
2. Understand how play can help children's learning or development.
3. Understand that play and activities should meet individual needs and avoid stereotyping and discrimination.

Teacher checklist

- ✓ Learners need to understand what the term 'positive' learning environment means
- ✓ Discuss the importance of play and how it can affect children if it is unsuitable

This unit has links with learning in Unit CFC2 Listening to and talking with a young child and Unit CFC9 Respecting and valuing children (these units are covered in Chapter 6 Communicating with children, TRP pages 81–94 and Student Book pages 96–109).

Additional guidance for delivery

Chapter 7 needs to be practical – playing with toys and reading to each other is a good way for learners to learn in this unit (making a story sack is a good practical activity). Keep a selection of toys that learners can sort into sets of suitable and unsuitable for different ages and stages of development. Use toy catalogues for pictures and ideas, e.g. Early Learning catalogues or Mothercare catalogues. Crucially, explore the importance of play and how it can affect children if it is unsuitable – for example board games that are too difficult.

Plan activities which support children's emotional development, for example, a painting activity where different types of music are played as the learners are painting works well (the paintings will alter).

When considering what a 'positive' learning environment means, encourage the learners to look at their own classroom – what would they like to change? Perhaps they could design a 'perfect' classroom.

Visits to settings are a very valuable experience too as many learners will not have been inside a day nursery before. It's important that the resources you use in this unit are similar to ones in the early years settings. Visits from play therapists (local hospital) are excellent as they give an insight into different work provision.

As a group, or on an individual basis, ask the learners to complete the interactive **Knowledge check** to finish the chapter.

Further resources

Pre-school Learning Alliance

Sure Start

www.playengland.org.uk/Page.asp

Play England provide resources and publications including Play Today magazine.

www.playwales.org.uk/

Play Wales is the Welsh national organisation for children's play.

www.literacytrust.org.uk/assets/0000/3210/Story_sack_guide.pdf

The National Literacy Trust – Story Sacks.

www.who.int/childgrowth/en/

The WHO Child Growth Standards – development norms from birth to 5 years old.

www.childdevelopmentinfo.com/development/normaldevelopment.shtml

A simplified overview of child development from birth to 5 years old.

www.nhs.uk/Tools/Pages/birthtofive.aspx?WT.srch=1&gclid=CNXD06LL_p8CFZBb4wodb2rkkA

An interactive guide to child development from birth to 5 years old.

Answers to activities

7.A1

Q	U	O	C	A	H	G	U	O	D	Y	A	L	P	E
D	Y	J	I	P	D	O	P	A	R	E	H	O	U	S
R	S	T	O	R	Y	T	I	M	E	T	O	O	T	I
E	S	W	A	T	R	I	P	L	A	T	M	P	N	A
S	A	H	S	E	N	D	R	O	S	A	E	L	E	R
S	E	E	C	O	N	F	I	D	E	N	C	E	M	P
I	Y	L	I	A	R	O	S	A	L	M	O	N	E	G
N	T	I	N	T	L	B	E	C	F	A	R	M	G	O
G	F	L	S	T	O	M	I	K	E	A	N	I	A	P
U	Z	S	A	O	Y	M	C	I	S	P	E	H	R	O
P	A	I	N	T	I	N	G	E	T	E	R	L	U	A
A	S	X	D	E	A	G	J	U	E	I	L	J	O	S
Y	A	L	P	E	V	I	T	A	E	R	C	O	C	O
G	H	U	O	D	C	I	S	U	M	O	S	A	N	B
S	T	O	O	H	T	M	I	E	V	I	T	A	E	C

Chapter 7 Play and learning

Overview of resources

Resources	Teaching notes	Link to Student Book	Link to Units and assessment criteria
7.A1 Play activities to build confidence	This activity can be used in several ways, the most obvious being a simple word search. To get more out of the sheet the learners can be given the words in advance and asked to consider how the activities listed could be used to build a child's confidence. Pair or small group work onto a flipchart with class feedback should generate ideas and the tutor may add points during feedback. As an extension the learners can write a sentence using each of the words.	p.112	**CFC1** *AC 1.1*
7.A2 The adult's role	Learners read each of the statements and decide how the adult should behave with regard to each, marking the ones that they feel are correct. Learners should be able to explain their reasons for their answers. The points can also be used as starting points for discussion work, e.g. how and when a playpen should be used.	p.113	**CFC1** *AC 1.2*
7.A3 Expressing emotions through play	This activity is designed to encourage learners to think about how children can express emotions through play. Learners should think about how different colours evoke different feelings, drawing faces into the circles to match the emotion that they are feeling. The second part of the activity sheet encourages the learners to consider age/stage appropriate activities of their own to allow children to express emotions through play. This could include puppets, a craft activity such as play dough or a story board. They should work in small groups to design an activity which they can carry out in class. Learners need to consider how the children would benefit from the activity and about confidence building and self-esteem. The sheet can also be extended to produce a wall display using paper plate faces and coloured hand prints, for puppets lolly sticks can be used in conjunction with the plates.	p.114	**CFC1** *AC 2.1*
7.A4 Thinking about self-esteem	This activity involves some self reflection; it may be useful to ask learners how they felt at school when they were praised or did well. Did they get good reports or win at anything? Alternatively, did they get into trouble or struggle to understand a particular subject – were they made to feel stupid or picked last for a team? They need to consider the effect that these things had on their own confidence and self-esteem. Has this affected their success and how they feel about their abilities today?	p.114	**CFC1** *AC 2.2*
7.A5 Susie's painting	This activity encourages learners to think about the impact that adults can have on a child and a child's self-esteem. This sheet can be used for discussion work or as an individual activity sheet.	p.114	**CFC1** *AC 1.2, 2.2*

Resources	Teaching notes	Link to Student Book	Link to Units and assessment criteria
7.A6 Treasure basket play	Learners think about a home-made treasure basket suitable for a baby over 6 months and the items that are safe to put in it. This session would be enhanced by taking in a basket with items that may or may not be suitable to use. Learners can handle the items themselves and put them into the basket. An extension of this may be to give learners themes and for them to suggest items for the basket, including how many items they should use.	p.116–17	**CFC5** AC 1.1
7.A7 Play in the home	Learners consider the value of playing with items available in the home. Pans and spoons are given as an example and this is matched up to learning outcomes. Learners should think about other activities that can be carried out using everyday items in the home, and state the benefits of the play. If the learners find this difficult, provide a few props (household items) or pictures of props for this session to stimulate ideas such as wash baskets for boats and clothes horses for dens. Learners need to consider health and safety.	p.116–17	**CFC5** AC 1.1
7.A8 Supporting play	Learners should understand that the adult role is important in supporting a child's play in the home. They should consider how the adults can extend the learning that is taking place. This worksheet encourages learners to look more closely at the types of play that they have suggested in Activity 7.A7 and consider the adult's role in supporting and encouraging the child.	p.118	**CFC 5** AC 2.1
7.A9 Adults' responsibilities	This worksheet consolidates learning. Learners should think about the responsibilities of the adult and make a list of these. Once they have accomplished this they can produce a poster showing the job of the adult when young children are playing	p.119	**CFC5** AC 2.2
7.A10 The ways children learn	This activity encourages learners to identify ways in which children learn. The session could be introduced with a thought shower to stimulate ideas in small groups or as a class activity. Learners then complete Activity 7.A10 individually or in pairs, depending on ability.	p.122–23	**CFC13** AC 1.1
7.A11 Rhymes and stories	Activity 7.A11 highlights how children can enjoy singing rhymes and songs with an adult. It illustrates the verbal and non-verbal communication between the children and the childcare practitioner. The learner could identify the skills that the children are learning such as following instructions, memory skills, social and emotional skills. Learners consolidate learning by writing three ways that you can encourage children to take part in songs and rhymes.	p.124–25	**CFC13** AC 2.1, 2.2, 2.3
7.A12 The natural world	Learners think about how the natural world can support children's learning. If learners find it difficult to think of other environments the tutor may give them some ideas such as seaside, countryside, park, etc. Learners should choose one example and plan an activity that encourages the child to learn about the natural world. Working individually or in pairs learners can produce activity sheets which can be put together to form a class book of activities. In groups or as a class the learners should discuss the points on the sheet.	p.126–27	**CFC13** AC 3.1, 3.2, 3.3

Resources	Teaching notes	Link to Student Book	Link to Units and assessment criteria
7.A13 Local community provisions	Learners explore how the local community can be used to broaden children's experiences. Learners begin with a research task to list local organisations that provide experiences for children. Learners then choose one item from their list and identify how that provision can support children's learning and development. An example of this has been given.	p.128–29	**CFC13** AC 4.1, 4.2. 4.3
7.H1 Play and development	The information here encourages the learner to focus on how play can help a baby to develop in many ways. Several activities are suggested at the end of the handout. When producing a mobile, it is important that the learners think about the position of the baby under the mobile, health and safety, colours, and the things they want to use to put it together.		**CFC17** AC 1.1, 3.2
7.A14 Individual needs	This activity encourages learners to consider appropriate ways that adults can help babies to play, learn and develop.	p.135	**CFC17** AC 1.2, 3.2
7.A15 Suitable toys and activities – birth to 15 months	Learners use toy catalogues (Mothercare/ELC/Boots, etc.) to select suitable toys and to write them into the appropriate age range on the sheet. This should be followed by discussion work to establish how a particular toy can help the development of the child	p.136–42	**CFC17** AC 2.1
7.A16 Benefits of activities	This consolidates learning as the learners now work individually to choose three of the toys that they have chosen in the previous task. They describe each one and the benefits to the child. An example has been given on the sheet.	p.143	**CFC17** AC 2.2
7.A17 Adults' role in safety	When buying toys it is important that they are safe. Learners should research safety marks and draw them onto the sheet. Learners need to think about other safety precautions that should be taken when babies and young children are playing. A table has been laid out for this activity which, once completed, can be used for discussion work with the group	p.144	**CFC 17** AC 3.1
7.A18 Positive learning environment	Learners look at the statements and identify which of them will contribute to a positive learning environment. This activity can be used as a springboard for further discussion, why should clothes pegs have personalised names on them or why shouldn't dressing-up clothes be on the floor, what would be a good alternative? An extension of this activity could be a written piece of work using the ideas for a poster.	p.148–51	**UPEL** AC 1.1, 1.2, 3.1
7.A19 Play develops skills	This is a matching activity where learners think about the benefits of particular activities. Some of the activities may have more than one benefit to the child. Discuss the answers with the group.	p.152	**UPEL** AC 2.1

Resources	Teaching notes	Link to Student Book	Link to Units and assessment criteria
Electronic resources			
7.PPT Play	This PowerPoint presentation provides a brief overview of why play is important and the resources and places which can be used in play.		
Knowledge Check	Interactive quiz covering learning from the units in the chapter for consolidation purposes. You could run the quiz via the VLE with learners during the first session to see how much they already know; it could be done again later to see how much progress they have made. Alternatively, more independent learners could have a go at completing the quiz on their own.		

7.A1 Play activities to build confidence

Find the following words in the word grid below:

ENCOURAGEMENT	SAND	CREATIVE PLAY
SELF-ESTEEM	PLAY DOUGH	HOME CORNER
PAINTING	MUSIC	DRESSING UP
PRAISE	STORY TIME	CONFIDENCE

Q	U	O	C	A	H	G	U	O	D	Y	A	L	P	E
D	Y	J	I	P	D	O	P	A	R	E	H	O	U	S
R	S	T	O	R	Y	T	I	M	E	T	O	O	T	I
E	S	W	A	T	R	I	P	L	A	T	M	P	N	A
S	A	H	S	E	N	D	R	O	S	A	E	L	E	R
S	E	E	C	O	N	F	I	D	E	N	C	E	M	P
I	Y	L	I	A	R	O	S	A	L	M	O	N	E	G
N	T	I	N	T	L	B	E	C	F	A	R	M	G	O
G	F	L	S	T	O	M	I	K	E	A	N	I	A	P
U	Z	S	A	O	Y	M	C	I	S	P	E	H	R	O
P	A	I	N	T	I	N	G	E	T	E	R	L	U	A
A	S	X	D	E	A	G	J	U	E	I	L	J	O	S
Y	A	L	P	E	V	I	T	A	E	R	C	O	C	O
G	H	U	O	D	C	I	S	U	M	O	S	A	N	B
S	T	O	O	H	T	M	I	E	V	I	T	A	E	C

On a separate piece of paper, write a sentence using each of the words.

CFC1

A.C. 1.2

7.A2 The adult's role

Read the statements below. Put a tick next to the statements which describe positive ways adults can support children while they gain confidence in an activity.

Make sure toys have a safety mark.	Leave child alone in a playpen.	Leave child alone in front of the television.
Go and have a bath while a baby is playing.	Be patient and repeat activities with the child.	Say 'well done' when a child completes an activity.
Supervise – always be with young babies when they play.	Chat to a friend on the phone while a child plays.	Make sure toys are suitable for the child's age.
Do not help the child.	Talk to the child about what they are doing.	Give a baby a toy which is suitable for a much older child.

7.A3 Expressing emotions through play

1. How do the colours of the rainbow below make you feel? Draw a face in each circle to show how each colour makes you feel.

   Here are some words which might be helpful:

sad	relaxed	frightened
angry	excited	energetic
happy	calm	cheerful

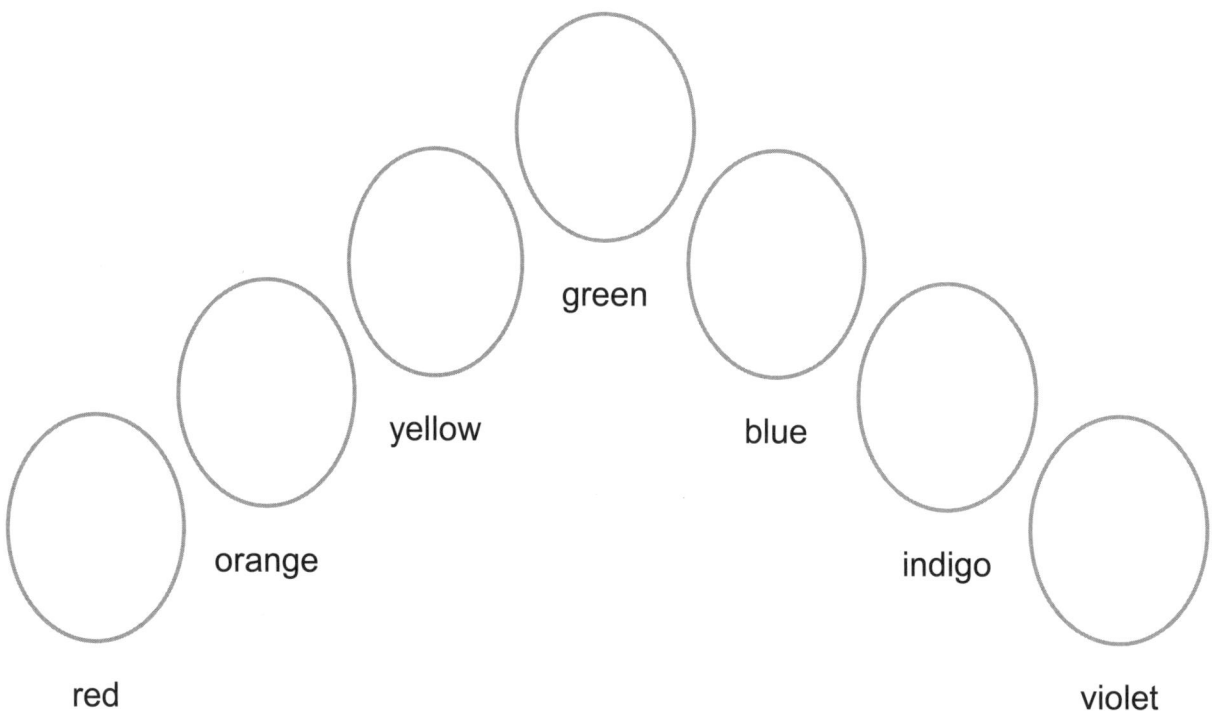

   green

   yellow

   blue

   orange

   indigo

   red

   violet

2. In small groups, discuss how you could use this activity to support a child to express their feelings.

3. On a separate piece of paper, list other activities which would support a child to express their feelings. Think about age-appropriate activities for both younger and older children. Some ideas for activities are craft, story or circle time.

4. Pick one activity you listed and make notes about the resources you would need. Make notes about how you would do the activity.

7.A4 Thinking about self-esteem

It is important that parents and carers help a child to feel valued. 'Valued' means loved, wanted and appreciated.

Think about what makes you feel good about yourself. It might be that your tutor has said that your work was excellent, or a friend has said that they like your new hairstyle.

Now think about what makes you feel bad about yourself. It might be that you find something difficult to do, or a friend has let you down.

1. List five things that give you high self-esteem, such as praise.

2. List five things that can make you have low self-esteem, such as being told you are stupid.

If you act in a positive way towards children, they will feel their efforts are valued – this leads to high self-esteem. Children who are always criticised may feel they are no good at anything and have low self-esteem.

7 Play and learning

CFC1
A.C. 1.2, 2.2

7.A5 Susie's painting

Susie has done a painting. Her mum and dad are both telling Susie what they think of it. Look at the speech bubbles below and think about how Susie might feel.

> What's that mess you've painted? It looks horrible!

Mum

> Wow! That's a brilliant painting. Well done!

Dad

1. In the chart below, write down the words that describe how Susie will feel:

   a) after her mum tells her what she thinks of the painting

   b) after her dad tells her what he thinks of the painting.

If you can think of any new words, add them to the chart. Here are some examples of words you might like to use:

upset	useless	good about herself
rewarded	ashamed	happy
successful	sad	encouraged
negative		

How does Susie's mum make her feel?	How does Susie's dad make her feel?

2. Now write two sentences to show which parent would have boosted Susie's self-esteem and which parent would have reduced it. Both sentences should contain the word 'because'.

Remember that a positive reaction from the adult means the child is ready to try again.

CFC5
A.C. 1.1

7.A6 Treasure basket play

You don't have to buy expensive toys – some household items can be used. Look at the items below. Which of them would be suitable to go into a treasure basket for a baby over six months? Draw lines from the items you would put in the basket.

piece of smooth wood

fir cone

keys

bar of soap

baby brush

sponge

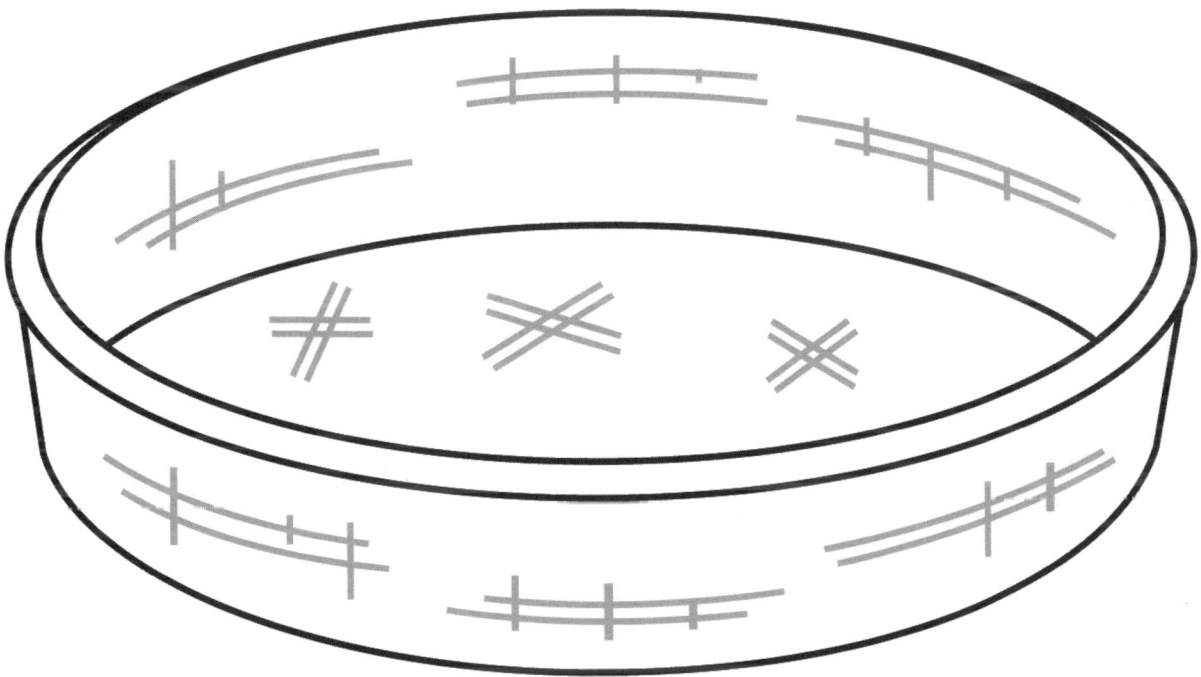

butter knife

flannel

long piece of silk ribbon

lavender bags

7.A7 Play in the home

Young children aged 1 to 2 years do not need expensive toys. They love to make noises. Playing with pans and wooden spoons is a great activity.

What other activities can be carried out at home using everyday items? Write a list in the table below in the left column. In the right column, list the benefits of each activity. An example has been given to help you.

Activity	Child's learning – benefits
Pans and spoons	Hand/eye coordination Social skills Rhythm

7.A8 Supporting play

1. List ways the adult can support a young child's play in the home. One has been completed as an example.

Activity	Adult support
Pans and wooden spoons	Sitting with the child to play Copying rhythm patterns Praising and encouraging

2. Below are some ideas for activities. How many more can you think of?

    - pairing socks
    - making the beds
    - helping to set the table
    - putting the shopping away

7.A9 Adults' responsibilities

1. In the spaces below, make a list of the responsibilities an adult has when a young child is playing. Two examples have been done for you.

Responsibilities
1. Make sure there is nothing sharp that the child can hurt themselves on.
2. Remember that children copy adults so be careful what you do in front of them.
3.
4.
5.
6.

2. Use the information in your list to design a poster to show adults what their responsibilities are.

CFC13
A.C. 1.1

7.A10 The ways children learn

Children learn in different ways. One way they can learn is by watching and copying. They watch the adults and children around them and then act out the things that they see.

Children also learn by trial and error, repeating actions and by discovering things.

Read the statements below. Draw lines to match each activity to the way the child is learning.

A baby is playing with a shape sorter toy. They try to put a shape in all the holes. The shape fits in one of the holes.	Watching and copying others
A child stacks bricks. They knock the bricks down. They then stack the bricks again.	Trial and error
A child helps to make a fruit juice ice lolly. When they take it out of the freezer they see it has frozen.	Repeating actions
A child is in the home corner of the nursery. They are pretending to make a cup of tea. Another child watches them and then joins in.	Discovery

7.A11 Rhymes and stories

1. Write a list of the rhymes and stories you know which are suitable for children from 0 to 5 years.

2. What sensory aids could you use when telling the story of Goldilocks and the Three Bears? Circle the items you would use.

bowl	dragon	teddy bears
goldfish	spoon	building blocks
seashell	table and chairs play furniture	
blonde doll		

3. Read the case study below and then answer the questions on a separate piece of paper.

> A group of 4 year olds are getting ready to sing 'Wind the bobbin up'. The childcare practitioner explains that they will sing it once with the words and actions, then hum it with actions and then finally do the actions without any sound. The children nod excitedly and the childcare practitioner smiles. He raises his hands ready to begin. The children are sitting on the carpet facing the practitioner so that he can make eye contact with each member of the group. During the activity the children are giggling. The childcare practitioner is smiling, nodding, clapping and telling the children, 'Well done'. At the end the children clap each other.

   a) Why it is important to include all of the children in the activity?

   b) How does the childcare practitioner control his group of children and get them to join in with the activity? Think about both verbal and non-verbal communication, for example hand gestures.

   c) Write in sentences three ways that you can encourage children to take part in songs and rhymes.

7.A12 The natural world

Natural environments let children discover the world they live in. Look at the example that has been completed for you.

1. List three more natural environments and suggest topics that can be used to extend children's experiences of the natural world.

Environment: The garden	**Environment:**
• Growing things: flowers, vegetables • The seasons: Spring, Summer, Autumn and Winter • A world of minibeasts, for example a wormery to produce compost • Birds: identification and feeding • Pets: caring for them	

Environment:	**Environment:**

2. Choose one example and plan an activity to encourage a child to learn about the natural world. Discuss the following:
   - How can the activity encourage a child to learn?
   - How can the activity extend a child's curiosity?
   - What health and safety measures would you need to put in place?

7.A13 Local community provisions

There are many local organisations, services and people which provide experiences for children.

1. Make a list in the space below of the organisations, services and people which provide experiences for children in your area. You could find them using some of the following resources:

   - Yellow Pages
   - local newspapers
   - Internet.

Organisations

2. Choose one organisation, service or person from your list. In the space below write down how it can broaden children's experiences. For example, children will learn about how other people live by meeting other children at Rainbows, Beavers or a toddler group.

_____ broadens children's experiences because

3. Using your ICT skills, create a leaflet for parents stating the benefits for children of finding out about their local community.

7.A14 Individual needs

Babies shouldn't be left to play on their own. Play helps babies to develop and it can help a baby's individual needs. Adults should provide the correct toys and activities to help the baby play. They should also join in play and encourage the baby.

Read about each baby below. Write down how an adult could support this baby's needs or encourage the baby to play. An example has been given for you.

Baby	To support and encourage play an adult should:
A baby who does not know how to use a new toy	• Show the baby how to use it • Repeat the action • Encourage the baby – talk about what they are doing • Make eye contact and smile
A baby who cries when it is left by its parent	
A baby who is learning to sit up	
A baby who is learning to walk	
A baby who needs help with their hand movements	

7.A15 Suitable toys and activities – birth to 15 months

Using toy catalogues (for example, Mothercare, Boots, ELC) write the names of suitable toys and play activities for each age of child in the spaces below.

Toys or play activities suitable for children aged…	
Birth to 3 months	**4 – 7 months**
8 – 11 months	**12 – 15 months**

CFC17
A.C. 2.2

7.A16 Benefits of activities

Choose three of the toys you listed on 7.A15.

In each box below:

- describe each toy/activity
- state the benefits to the baby of each toy/activity

If you have time, find a photo or picture of each toy and stick it next to each toy.

An example has been given for you.

Toy	Cot toy fixed to the side of the cot
Activity	Babies make noises by hitting buttons, rolling wheels, twisting switches and ringing bells.
Benefit	All this develops fine motor and gross motor skills which helps baby to learn to control its movements.

Toy 1	
Activity	
Benefit	

Toy 2	
Activity	
Benefit	

Toy 3	
Activity	
Benefit	

7.A17 Adults' role in safety

Safety marks mean that toys meet certain regulations, making sure that they are safe. All toys should have a safety mark on them.

1. Using the Internet or childcare books, find and draw the safety marks used.

Safety marks found on toys

2. Think about other safety precautions that should be taken when babies and young children are playing.

Action	Explanation
Supervision	Always make sure that children are well supervised when they are playing.
Age/stage appropriate	
Amount of toys out at one time	
Safety marks	
Second-hand equipment	

UPEL

A.C. 1.1, 1.2, 3.1

7.A18 Positive learning environment

1. Read the following statements. Put a tick next to the features that will contribute to a positive learning environment. Put a cross next to the features which will not contribute to a positive learning environment.

Feature	Tick or cross	Feature	Tick or cross
Farm animal toys and play people		Jigsaws with pieces missing	
Parents' noticeboard		Celebrating different festivals and cultures	
Children left in front of the television		No books	
Construction sets, e.g. Lego®		Pretend telephone, kitchen and till	
Children are given a snack if they are hungry		Dirty toilets	
Empty display boards		Bright displays	
Welcome sign in many languages		Sand and water on the floor	
Dressing-up clothes on the floor in the home corner		Too many children around the craft table	

2. Choose two of the features you ticked. In the space below, give one reason why these features might help a child to learn.

UPEL

A.C. 2.1

7.A19 Play develops skills

Match each activity to the area of development it helps children to learn. Do some of the activities support more than one area of development?

Talking with a friend	
Bead threading	**Physical**
Role play and dressing up	
Small world play	
Construction play	**Social**
Riding a tricycle	
Board games	
Pouring and measuring water	**Emotional**
Box modelling	
Painting	
Building dens	**Intellectual**
Pretending to talk on a play phone	
Stories	
Peek-a-boo	**Language**
Singing songs	

CFC17

A.C. 1.1, 3.2

7.H1 Play and development

Babies like to play and play supports babies' development.

Physical development

Babies try to grasp toys and fingers if offered. This helps them develop their hand movements. Playing peek-a-boo also helps this. Hand movements are also called fine manipulative skills.

Large movements are called gross motor skills. Large movements can be encouraged by hanging a mobile above the baby's cot – the baby must stretch up to reach it. Musical toys encourage babies to kick and stretch.

Social and emotional development

By making eye contact with babies you are helping them to copy and develop an important social skill. Smiling at babies when interacting with them is also important. Babies need to trust people who look after them: this is called bonding.

Play is important to introduce babies to social development. Even babies have to learn that they can't have everything their own way. A baby sitting in a highchair might 'accidentally' drop a toy onto the floor – the adult picks it up – the baby gets attention so drops it again and again. However, they have to learn that the carer will not always pick up the toy.

Intellectual and language development

Babies need to have adult attention to stimulate learning. Adults must sing and talk to babies to encourage intellect (memory skills and thinking skills). Play stimulates learning too. For example, encouraging babies to play with stacking blocks and shape sorters helps them to learn about shape and size.

It is essential to talk to babies so that they can hear and recognise words. If an adult points to objects while saying the word, this will help the baby to learn and develop language.

Suggested activities:

- Design a mobile suitable for a baby.
- Make a list of suitable toys for a baby to have in a high chair.
- Make a list of nursery rhymes that are suitable for young babies.

Introduction

This chapter covers:

L1 CFC21 Science activities for young children

L1 CFC23 Musical activities for young children

Helping young children to explore and discover is a very important aspect of their development. Understanding how activities and science can be linked will enable the learners to provide valuable activities for children.

Young children also enjoy rhythm, movement and singing. Musical activities or games provide more than just fun – they give the young child a chance to express themselves. It also introduces key concepts such as counting, position (up, down, in, out, etc.), and parts of the body, as well as contributing to physical development. Very young children will often automatically enjoy banging so if learners can provide stimulating musical activities or games, it will help the child/children's all round development.

It is suggested that you tackle the music unit with learners first.

Learning outcomes

Unit CFC21

Unit CFC21 has three learning outcomes:

1. Know science activities suitable for young children.
2. Know how to set up science activities to support the young child's learning.
3. Know the learning which young children can gain from science activities.

> **Teacher checklist**
> - ✓ Describe science activities suitable for children aged 18 months to 2 years and for children aged between 3 to 5 years
> - ✓ List the science resources needed to carry out these activities
> - ✓ Be aware of possible health and safety risks associated with these activities
> - ✓ Know how to support a child when carrying out specific science activities
> - ✓ Describe the learning a child would gain from these activities
> - ✓ Stress the importance of health and safety at all times

Unit CFC23

Unit CFC23 has two learning outcomes:

1. Know the benefits of musical activities for young children.
2. Know how to make musical activities or musical games for young children.

> **Teacher checklist**
> - ✓ List musical activities for babies under 6 months, young children aged 1 to 2 years and children aged 3 to 5 years
> - ✓ Know the benefits for children of these activities
> - ✓ Describe how to make musical activities or games
> - ✓ Know the value of these activities and games
> - ✓ Identify the learning that children receive through these activities and games

Additional guidance for delivery

Some learners might feel uncomfortable during some of the practical musical activities – your enthusiasm will help them to overcome this. An introduction to different types of suitable instruments is also a good ice breaker. (You will find some good music boxes in educational catalogues.)

In small groups, encourage the learners to list nursery rhymes that they already know and then feed back to the whole group. This can help to boost learners' self-esteem as it gives them a starting point.

As a starting point to the science unit, discuss the ways in which children explore by using the five senses. Do the learners know what these are? Learners could start by producing a poster showing the five senses.

Show learners how to evaluate activities via simple reflections on what they may change next time. Learners could think of ways they could evidence their findings and produce their own worksheets.

Encourage learners to take photos and to print them – they can use them to record results and evidence in the format of basic journals.

In addition to the activities, and if time allows, learners could make 'touchy feely' bags where they wear a blindfold, put their hands in a bag or box and try to guess what object they have in their hand. They could also create 'smell pots' – yoghurt pots covered with paper with a few holes in the top, covering different things like coffee grains, toothpaste, orange peel, etc.

As a group, or on an individual basis, ask the learners to complete the interactive **Knowledge check** to finish the chapter.

Further resources

www.sparklebox.co.uk

Sparklebox has a wealth of educational resources, many of which are free to download.

http://www.practicalpreschool.com

Practical Pre-School magazine is a useful resource for those working with children in the Early Years Foundation Stage.

http://education.scholastic.co.uk/child_education

The website for Child Education Plus has some inspirational resources for music and science topics.

www.makingfriends.com/musical_instruments.htm

A useful website when learners are making musical instruments.

Chapter 8 Activities for children

Overview of resources

Resources	Teaching notes	Link to Student Book	Link to Units and assessment criteria
8.A1 Science activities for young children	Learners need to consider suitable science activities. They should also think about health and safety implications, for example when baking children may have nut allergies, or be sensitive to soap products. In groups learners should think about the suitability of each activity, what each activity may involve, and the health and safety measures that should be put in place to protect young children taking part in the activities. Four of these points should be written into the box provided.	p.168–71	**CFC21** AC 1.1, 2.2
8.A2 Water and ice	This activity guides the learners through planning a science activity for 18 months to 2 year olds. Working in small groups the learners consider the four points and make notes to feed back to the rest of the class.	p.168	**CFC21** AC 1.2, 2.1, 2.2, 2.3, 3.1
8.A3 Plan a science activity	This activity is an extension of 8.A2. Learners need to plan their own activities for 18 months to 2 year olds and 3 to 5 year olds. Learners might want to choose one of the suitable examples from Activity 8.A1. Where possible the learners should carry out the activities and evaluate their success; this can be done in placement or with their peer group participating. If the learner peer group are involved they could also evaluate learning. The activities can be made into a booklet for the class.	p.168–71	**CFC21** AC 1.2, 2.1, 2.2, 2.3, 3.1
8.A4 Growing plants	This activity introduces the many different types of seeds and bulbs that can be used to teach children about growing and planting. The learners plan an activity sheet that a child can follow using pictures and where possible photos. The activity encourages learners to consider the different materials that can be used for this, for example some allow the children to study the root growth, and the equipment needed for this type of activity (e.g. a watering can). Learners should consider health and safety when planning activities. This would also be a good opportunity to incorporate song and rhymes such as 'Five little peas in a peapod pressed' or 'Dingle dangle scarecrow'. Extension activities such as drawing the stages of plant growth or a sunflower race where learners log height over a period of time, will show learners how learning opportunities can be included in their planning.		**CFC21** AC 1.2, 2.1, 2.2

Resources	Teaching notes	Link to Student Book	Link to Units and assessment criteria
8.A5 Rhymes and songs	Learners consider how music helps with children's development. A discussion prior to completing Activity 8.A5 can be done as a class activity or in small groups. Examples of different styles of music, songs and instruments will extend this activity and generate ideas. The activity gives learners a chance to make their own nursery rhyme book (to include a minimum of five rhymes). This should be produced on a computer and needs to be spellchecked (an opportunity for ICT).	p.174–79	**CFC23** *AC 1.1*
8.A6 Musical activities	Learners need to think about which musical instruments and activities are suitable for different aged children. It also asks for thoughts about what children will learn through the activity.	p.174–79	**CFC23** *AC 1.1, 1.2*
8.A7 The benefits of musical activities	Learners think about the benefits of music. A thought shower would generate ideas for the learners to use to complete the table.	p.174–79	**CFC23** *AC 1.2*
8.A8 Music and development	Learners consider how music helps with children's development. A discussion prior to completing the activity sheet can be done as a class activity or in small groups. Examples of different styles of music, songs and instruments will extend this activity and generate ideas.	p.174–79	**CFC23** *AC 1.2, 2.2, 2.3*
8.A9 Home-made instruments	Activity 8.A9 guides the learners towards making their own musical instrument. It encourages them to think about the materials that they will need and the health and safety considerations they should consider during the planning of their activity. Remind them of basic issues such as securely fixing the tops on home-made rattles. Also issue a caution that kidney beans are poisonous and should not be used. Once they have made their instrument, the learners should plan an activity that is suitable for children. They can share this with the group either as a presentation or a demonstration. Their presentation could include information about how it will help with a child's development (a consolidation of Activity 8.A8).		**CFC23** *AC 2.1*

Resources	Teaching notes	Link to Student Book	Link to Units and assessment criteria
Electronic resources			
8.PPT1 Science activities	8.PPT1 introduces the topic of science activities and their benefits for children. The presentation explores how children use their five senses to learn and the adult's role in ensuring activities are carried out safely.		
8.PPT2 Musical activities	8.PPT2 introduces learners to different types of musical activities and how they can benefit children's development (e.g. number skills, fine motor skills, etc.).		
Knowledge Check	Interactive quiz covering learning from the units in the chapter for consolidation purposes. You could run the quiz via the VLE with learners during the first session to see how much they already know; it could be done again later to see how much progress they have made. Alternatively, more independent learners could have a go at completing the quiz on their own.		

8.A1 Science activities for young children

1. Circle science activities that are suitable for young children.

Sinking and floating	Dry and wet sand
Using buttons of different sizes	Soap and water
Water and ice	Planting
Mixing chemicals	Weather charts
Measuring puddles	Baking/cookery
Mixing powder paint	

2. It is really important that all science activities are safe and suitable for children. Think carefully and list four points to remember when doing science activities with young children.

1.

2.

3.

4.

8.A2 Water and ice

A suitable activity for children aged 18 months to 2 years is exploring how water changes to ice in the freezer.

water + juice + ice lolly mould + freezer = ice lolly you can eat

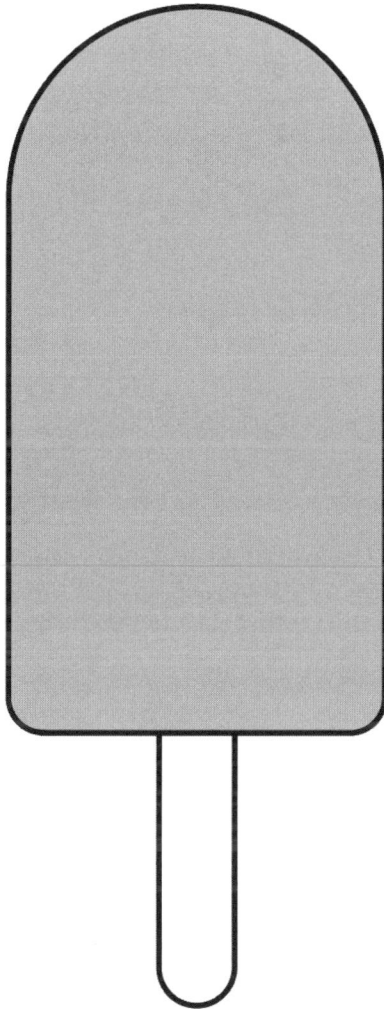

This activity is really easy to do with young children. The biggest problem is how long they have to wait until they can eat the lolly!

In small groups, list on a separate piece of paper:

1. What resources do you need to do this activity?
2. What health and safety issues do you need to think about?
3. What is the role of the adult working with children in this activity?
4. What would children learn from doing this activity?

Share your responses with the rest of the group.

8.A3 Plan a science activity

Plan your own science activity for a child aged 18 months to 2 years. (Look at A8.1 for ideas.) You can use this sheet to make notes.

- What resources will you need?

- What health and safety issues should you consider?

- What will the adult's role be?

- What do you want the children to learn from this activity?

- If you get a chance to carry out this activity, try to evaluate it. (This means you say how the activity went, what you would do differently and if the children learned what you hoped they would.)

Using the above headings, plan an activity for a child aged 3 to 5 years. You can do this on a separate sheet.

8.A4 Growing plants

1. Choose one of the following:

sunflower seed	cress
mung beans	runner bean
amaryllis/daffodil bulb	lettuce
radish	peas
courgette	strawberry

2. You are going to produce an activity sheet for a child under 5.

   Use illustrated checklists which show the materials that will be needed, for example, plant pot and equipment (e.g. trowel).

   Step by step photographs will show children what to do at each stage of the activity.

3. Think about health and safety – wear an apron and cover your work space with newspaper

4. Now plan follow up activities:
   * Think about suitable songs.
   * Can you eat the end product?
   * Could the growing process be recorded by drawings or charts?
   * Consider aftercare and watering.
   * Preparing food, for example egg and cress sandwiches.

CFC23

A.C. 1.1

8.A5 Rhymes and songs

Look at the following nursery rhymes and songs. Think about the three age ranges given; which rhymes and songs would be the most suitable for the different age ranges?

1. Match the ages to the rhymes and songs by drawing a line to link the title to the appropriate age

Under 6 months	Pat a Cake Pat a Cake
	The Farmer's in His Den
	Miss Polly
1–2 years	London's Burning (rounds)
	Round and Round the Garden
	Peter Piper
3–5 years	I'm a Little Teapot
	This Little Piggy
	Five Little Speckled Frogs

2. You are going to make a book: Choose one of the age ranges and think of at least two more suitable rhymes or songs for that age range. Put together a child's song book which includes words and illustrations. You can now share this with your group.

8.A6 Musical activities

Look at the table below. For each age group write down suitable instruments and activities. Also write down how the instrument or activity can benefit a child's development and learning.

In the box below are some ideas which may help you. You might use some words more than once. You might think of your own words too.

wrist shaker	coconut halves
counting rhymes	hand-eye coordination
rasp	use as part of a song or rhyme
triangle	movement
musical statues	tambourine
homemade shaker	dancing
fine manipulative skills	listening skills
drums	lullabies
learning about sound	rhythm
singing songs	enjoyment
encourages listening skills	imitation

Age	Instruments and activities	Child's learning
Under 6 months	e.g. Rattle	e.g. Gross motor skills
1–2 years		
3–5 years		

8.A7 The benefits of musical activities

Musical activities help children learn. Complete the table below by writing down how musical activities help children learn each skill or ability. An example has already been given.

Skill or ability	How
Confidence	
Self-esteem	
Language development	
Hand to eye coordination	
Body control	
Counting	Children learn to count through nursery rhymes like 'Five currant buns in a baker's shop' or 'Five little ducks went swimming one day'
Social skills	
Volume control	

8.A8 Music and development

Music helps children's development. Can you fill in the boxes below? There is an example to get you started.

Activity	How activity helps development
Movement to music	Moving to music helps with coordination and balance. Gross motor skills are enhanced by dancing to music. It helps the child to become aware of the space around them too.
Banging a drum	
Action and finger rhymes	
Hokey Cokey	

8.A9 Home-made instruments

What kind of instrument are you going to make?

1. Think about the materials you will need. Look at the words below and cross out any materials that are unsuitable.

glass jars	plastic bottle	pulses, e.g. lentils
red kidney beans	gloss paint	sticky tape
yoghurt pots	pasta shapes	nails and screws

2. Think about health and safety issues, both in the making of the instrument and when children use it. List them below.

3. Think of an activity you could do with children, using your instrument, and share this with the rest of your group.

Introduction

This chapter covers:

E3 CFC8 Contraception information

E3 CFC6 Responsibilities of new parent(s)

This chapter will help the learner to understand the different methods of contraception available and the strengths and weaknesses of each. Advice is also given on where to go for help and guidance when sexually active, including information on sexually transmitted infections (STIs).

Caring for a baby is a big responsibility and this chapter goes on to explore issues around pregnancy and the care of a very young baby. These include the stages of a baby's growth and development during pregnancy, how to support a mum-to-be during pregnancy, the roles and responsibilities of new parents and how to look after a new baby for the first 12 weeks of life.

Learning outcomes

Unit CFC8

Unit CFC8 has two learning outcomes:

1. Know about contraception.
2. Know where to seek advice in relation to contraception.

> **Teacher checklist**
> ✓   Know the range of contraceptives available and how to use them
> ✓   Know the strengths and weaknesses of each type of contraceptive
> ✓   Does the chosen contraceptive protect against sexually transmitted disease?
> ✓   Where can learners go for confidential contraceptive advice?
> ✓   What about the pregnancy myths – fact or fiction?

Unit CFC6

Unit CFC6 has three learning outcomes:

1. Know about a baby's growth and development during pregnancy.
2. Understand the care required for a mum during pregnancy.
3. Know the support available to new parent(s).

> **Teacher checklist**
> ✓   Know about the baby's development and state the stages from conception to birth
> ✓   Know about the care required for a mum-to-be during pregnancy
> ✓   What factors could affect the unborn baby?
> ✓   What support might parents need during the first 12 weeks of their baby's life?
> ✓   Where can support be obtained for a) the new baby, b) the new mum and c) the new parents?

Additional guidance for delivery

Before you deliver this chapter, and the advice on contraception and STIs, it is useful to put together several packs which include leaflets (e.g. from the FPA (Family Planning Association)) and samples of the different types of contraception available. Learners are then encouraged to put together their own collection of leaflets and fact sheets (advising them, for example, of where they could go to for local contraceptive advice).

Invite speakers to visit and to support the learners, for example, local sexual health advisers. You could also ask a local health visitor or midwife to visit, or even a new mum and her baby.

As a group, or on an individual basis, ask the learners to complete the interactive **Knowledge check** to finish the chapter.

Further resources

www.fpa.org.uk/homepage

Helpful advice from the Family Planning Association.

www.choices4u.org.uk/

Advice on contraception and sexual health.

www.brook.org.uk/

Brook clinics offer confidential advice for people under 25 years of age, tel. no. 0808 802 123.

www.nhs.uk

This website provides support offered by the National Health Service.

www.nhscareers.nhs.uk/details/Default.aspx?Id=807

Visit this website for details of careers within the NHS.

www.education.gov.uk

Visit this website and follow the links in the children and young people section for further details of initiatives.

www.citizensadvice.org.uk/

Visit this website to access the Citizens Advice Bureau online support and information.

www.gingerbread.org.uk/content/354/Your-family

The website for Gingerbread, a national charity which provides support and advice for single parents.

Babette Cole, *Mummy laid an egg,* ISBN 978-0-099-29911-0 Good support when learners are tackling Activity 9.A5.

Answers to activities

9.A5

Unprotected sexual intercourse – sperm enters cervix after ejaculation – sperm meets egg in fallopian tube, embryo formed – embryo wafted into womb (uterus) – missed period – 4 weeks, heart as big as a poppy seed – pregnancy confirmed by doctor – by week 8, now called a foetus, looks like a baby – 3 months, foetus begins to move although the mother cannot feel it yet – 5 months, foetus is about 15 cm long, hair is starting to grow – 7 months, foetus sleeps and wakes at regular intervals, it can blink – 39 weeks, all organs are fully developed (the last being the lungs) – 40 weeks, birth

9.A8

Across: 2. pregnancy; 3. shellfish; 5. fertilisation; 6. midwife; 8. ovulation; 10. umbilical cord

Down: 1. birth; 3. sperm; 4. health visitor; 5. foetus; 7. diet; 9. uterus

9.A10

R	E	S	P	O	N	S	I	B	I	L	I	T	Y	A
Q	W	E	O	N	D	I	N	U	M	U	M	R	A	B
N	E	O	N	I	P	D	A	D	A	P	L	A	L	I
B	O	N	D	I	N	G	M	G	N	O	P	I	P	L
O	B	E	I	L	K	Y	E	E	U	A	M	G	L	I
N	S	R	P	R	I	N	B	T	O	I	L	K	B	T
F	G	N	I	S	I	L	A	I	C	O	S	S	H	Y
E	P	X	O	T	A	L	L	Y	U	O	H	A	N	D
S	A	F	E	T	Y	O	L	O	D	P	E	K	D	E
K	L	S	A	F	O	I	Y	E	D	A	L	F	R	N
A	Z	O	M	C	M	P	B	E	L	A	T	R	A	I
H	A	P	P	A	R	N	E	D	E	N	E	I	G	T
A	I	M	F	A	M	V	I	O	S	A	R	J	P	U
N	I	G	H	T	F	E	E	D	S	O	F	L	O	O
M	Y	S	S	E	N	I	L	N	A	E	L	C	L	R

9.A11

- Midwife – 5 and 8
- Health visitor – 2 and 10
- Gingerbread – 3 and 7
- Citizens Advice Bureau – 4 and 9
- Sure Start – 1 and 6

Chapter 9 Parenting

Overview of resources

Resources	Teaching notes	Link to Student Book	Link to Units and assessment criteria
9.A1 Types of contraceptive	In order to understand the different types of contraception, learners need to understand the different methods available, how they work and where they can go to for contraceptive advice. Activities 9.A1 and 9.A2 will help them to do this.	p.186–87	**CFC8** *AC 1.1, 1.2, 2.1, 2.2*
9.A2 Researching contraceptives	Before you deliver 9.A2, put together six packs, each containing a named picture of one of the contraceptives shown on 9.A1. Include a sample if possible, e.g. a condom and an up-to-date booklet on the contraceptive from the Family Planning Association. Learners then work individually or in groups to look at one pre-prepared pack and complete the fact sheet on 9.A2. They then feed back to the rest of the class.		
9.A3 Pregnancy myths	Encourage the learners to work in pairs to think about the myths of pregnancy and to discuss the reality of the statements. Each pair can be invited to read out one of their responses and to give their reason for it being a fact or a myth (list them on the whiteboard under a myth or fact heading). The class can agree or disagree. If they disagree they should give their reasons for this. Make sure you give the correct answers to any myths or facts that are misinterpreted. Learners can also be encouraged to put forward any statements that they have heard themselves and are not sure about.		**CFC8** *AC 2.1*
9.A4 Sexually transmitted infections	This is a tutor-led activity. Before the class arrive, prepare the flashcards and draw a 2-column table on the whiteboard with headings 'viral' and 'bacterial'. Give one card to each learner and ask them to consider whether 'their infection' is bacterial or viral. (Explain that bacterial infections are treatable and recovery is usual but that viral infections, although treatable, remain in the body and can recur. Viral infections are not curable, e.g. HIV which can develop into AIDS.) Learners say the name of 'their infection' and if it is bacterial or viral and give any information that they know, e.g. chlamydia can lead to infertility. Fill in any gaps in information to a level suitable for the group. This activity encourages learners to consider the implications of unprotected sex (sex without the use of a condom) and to divide STIs into two groups, viral and bacterial. It allows the learners to discuss the implications of contracting a sexually transmitted infection.		**CFC8** *AC 1.2*

Resources	Teaching notes	Link to Student Book	Link to Units and assessment criteria
9.A5 Pregnancy timeline	Learners need to know the stages from conception to birth. The cards in this activity can be used in a number of ways: learners can each be given a card and then organise themselves into a 'human' timeline; alternatively the learners can work individually or in small groups to put the line together as a cut and paste activity which can then be kept in their files for reference. Both activities can be used together to create a discussion and then a follow-up task to check learning.	p.192–93	**CFC6** AC 1.1
9.A6 Good practice during pregnancy	This activity helps learners to begin to identify how a mum-to-be should care for herself and her unborn child. The activity requires the learner to tick the good points or put a cross against the bad points. An extension of this activity would be to write a sentence about each point.	p.194–95	**CFC6** AC 2.1
9.A7 Factors that could harm an unborn baby	Individually, learners are encouraged to think more carefully about factors that could harm the unborn baby by placing a tick against beneficial factors and a cross against potentially harmful activities. Learners then discuss their answers. Alternatively, you can use Activity 9.A7 to make several sets of cards. Then make two large circles – a red one (harmful) and a green one (beneficial). Distribute the cards and ask the learners to place their cards in the correct circle. Learners could then discuss their answers as a group (fill in any gaps where learners are unsure). To check learning, this could be followed by a pairs game where each learner turns over two cards and, if the cards match, they must say why they are harmful or beneficial for the mum-to-be. If they are correct they keep the cards and score a point; if the cards don't match, or they cannot answer, the cards are turned back over and the next learner turns over two more cards.	p.195	**CFC6** AC 2.2
9.A8 Parenting crossword puzzle	This crossword puzzle is a fun consolidation task to check learning of the unit so far.		**CFC6** AC 1.1, 1.2, 2.2
9.A9 Buying baby equipment	This activity encourages learners to think about the needs of a new baby and the items that it requires. Adding the element of numeracy in the form of a budget encourages learners to think about the cost involved in purchasing things for a baby. Learners should use catalogues or the Internet to find and price the items that they feel are necessary, keeping within their budget allocation. Class feedback can be used to discuss what the learners feel the baby cannot do without.		**CFC6** AC 3.1
9.A10 New parent responsibilities	Learners complete the word search; an extension of this activity could be to contextualise the words by putting them into sentences.		**CFC6** AC 3.1

Resources	Teaching notes	Link to Student Book	Link to Units and assessment criteria
9.A11 Support for parents **9.H1** Family support	It is essential that learners have some knowledge about the support that is available to new parents. This activity covers five support agencies who can offer support to parents throughout birth and during the first 12 weeks. Learners connect two statements to each of the support agencies. It can be used in conjunction with Handout 9.H1 as a comprehension task. An extension to this would be to ask learners to complete further research about one or more of the support agencies and report back to the group to share information gathered.	p.196–97	**CFC6** AC 3.1, 3.2
Electronic resources			
9.PPT1 Contraception **9.PPT2** Pregnancy	9.PPT1 introduces the different types of contraception that are available and discusses their use in preventing pregnancy and protecting against sexually transmitted diseases (STIs). 9.PPT2 introduces the topics of conception and pregnancy. It looks at factors that could harm an unborn baby and sources of support for new parents.		
Knowledge Check	Interactive quiz covering learning from the units in the chapter for consolidation purposes. You could run the quiz via the VLE with learners during the first session to see how much they already know; it could be done again later to see how much progress they have made. Alternatively, more independent learners could have a go at completing the quiz on their own.		

CFC8

AC 1.1, 1.2, 2.1, 2.2

9.A1 Types of contraceptive

Match the types of contraception to the correct pictures.

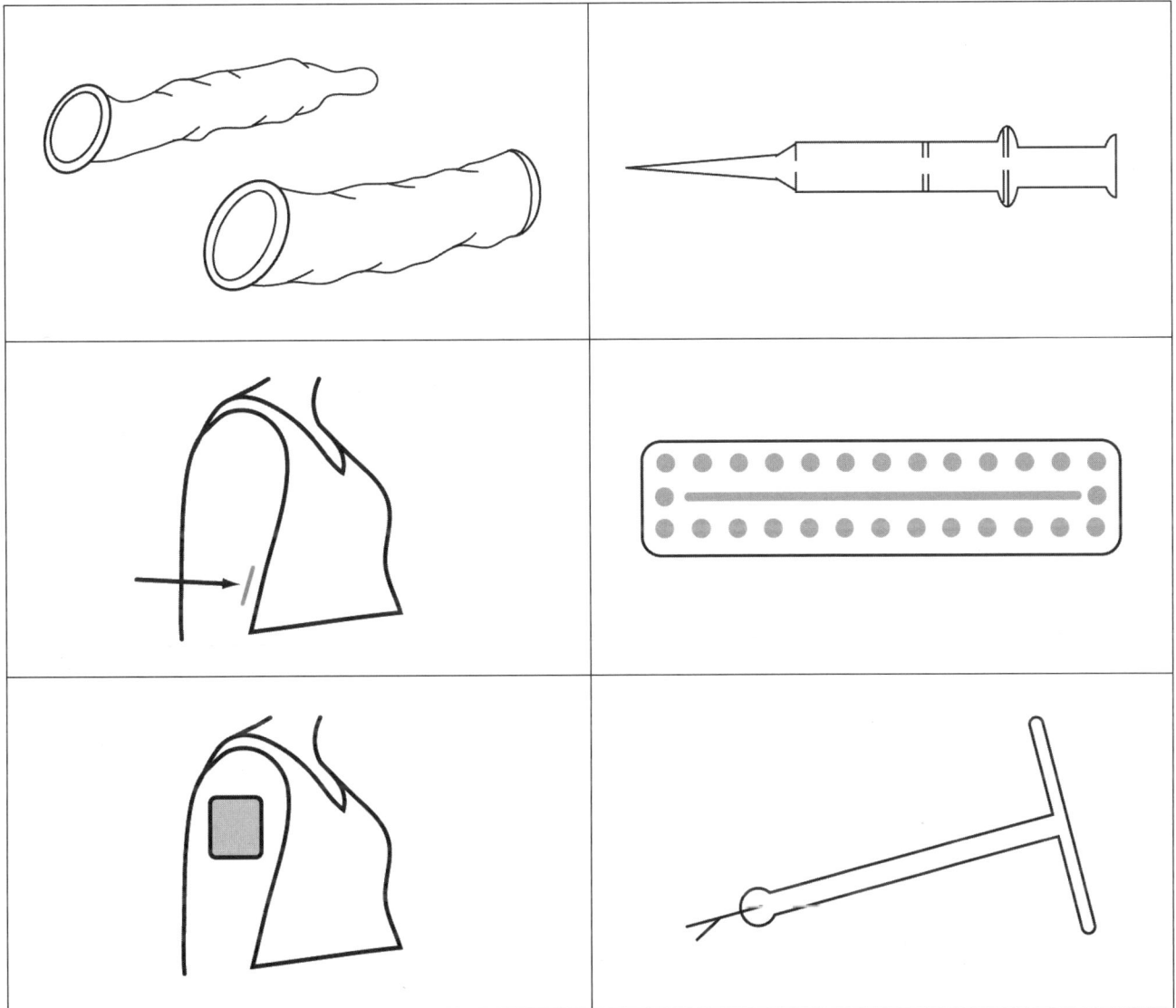

contraceptive injection	implant
IUD (coil)	contraceptive patch
contraceptive pill	male and female condoms

CFC8
AC 1.1, 1.2, 2.1, 2.2

9.A2 Researching contraception

Use the pack your tutor gives you to research one contraceptive.
Complete this fact sheet with your findings.

What method of contraception are you researching?
How does it prevent pregnancy?
List the strengths of this type of contraceptive.
List the weaknesses of this type of contraceptive.
Does it protect against sexually transmitted infections?
Who can you go to to get contraceptive advice?

9.A3 Pregnancy myths

With a partner, discuss each of these statements. Decide whether each one is a fact or a myth. Give a reason for your decision.

Statement	Myth or fact?	Why?
You can't get pregnant if the man withdraws before ejaculation.		
You can get pregnant if you have never had intercourse before and this is your first time.		
You can't get pregnant if you are breast feeding.		
You can get pregnant if the man has just had a vasectomy.		
You can't get pregnant if you have never had a period.		
You can get pregnant if you are taking antibiotics when you are on the pill.		
You can't get pregnant if you have intercourse standing up.		
You can get pregnant if you are on your period.		

CFC8
AC 1.2

9.A4 Sexually transmitted infections (STIs)

For tutor use – flashcard activity

Create flashcards using the statements below. Give one card to each learner. Ask each learner to put their flashcard under the correct heading written on the whiteboard: bacterial or viral.

Please refer to information in the Overview of resources, page 140.

Chlamydia	Gonorrhoea	Syphilis
Herpes 1 and 2	Genital warts	Hepatitis
HIV	Parasites	Candida (thrush)
Papilloma virus	Trichomoniasis	

CFC6
AC 1.1

9.A5 Pregnancy timeline

Work in pairs or groups to put these statements in the correct order.

Unprotected sexual intercourse	4 weeks – heart as big as a poppy seed	Missed period	5 months – foetus is about 15 cm long, hair is starting to grow
Sperm meets egg in fallopian tube, embryo forms	Embryo wafted into womb (uterus)	7 months – foetus sleeps and wakes at regular intervals, it can blink	40 weeks – birth
Pregnancy confirmed by doctor	Sperm enters cervix after ejaculation	Week 8 – now called a foetus, looks like a baby	39 weeks - all organs are fully developed, the last being the lungs
3 months – foetus begins to move although the mother cannot feel it yet			

9.A6 Good practice during pregnancy

Read the statements below.

Put a tick next to things which you think are good practice for a pregnant woman. Put a cross next to things which you think are not good or safe practice for a pregnant woman.

	Tick or cross		Tick or cross
Rest during the daytime		Eat a healthy diet	
Take up a new sport		Go on fairground rides	
Get stressed		Sit with feet raised	
Party all night		Smoke 20 cigarettes a day	
Get 8 hours sleep each night		Drink milk	
Go to antenatal classes		Drink a bottle of wine each night	
Take medication not prescribed by her doctor		Eat twice the amount she normally eats	

CFC6
AC 2.2

9.A7 Factors that could harm an unborn baby

Look at the factors below. Put a tick against the ones that would be good for an unborn baby and a cross against the ones that would be bad for it.

antenatal care	gentle exercise	fruit	cat litter tray
vegetables	folic acid	mum-to-be resting with her feet up and reading to a toddler	walking
rest	a mum-to-be with family (support)	alcohol	pregnant woman horse riding
cigarette	soft cheese, pâté, tuna, shellfish	sheep on a farm	antenatal classes
cup of coffee	illegal drugs	prescribed drugs	paint

9.A8 Parenting crossword puzzle

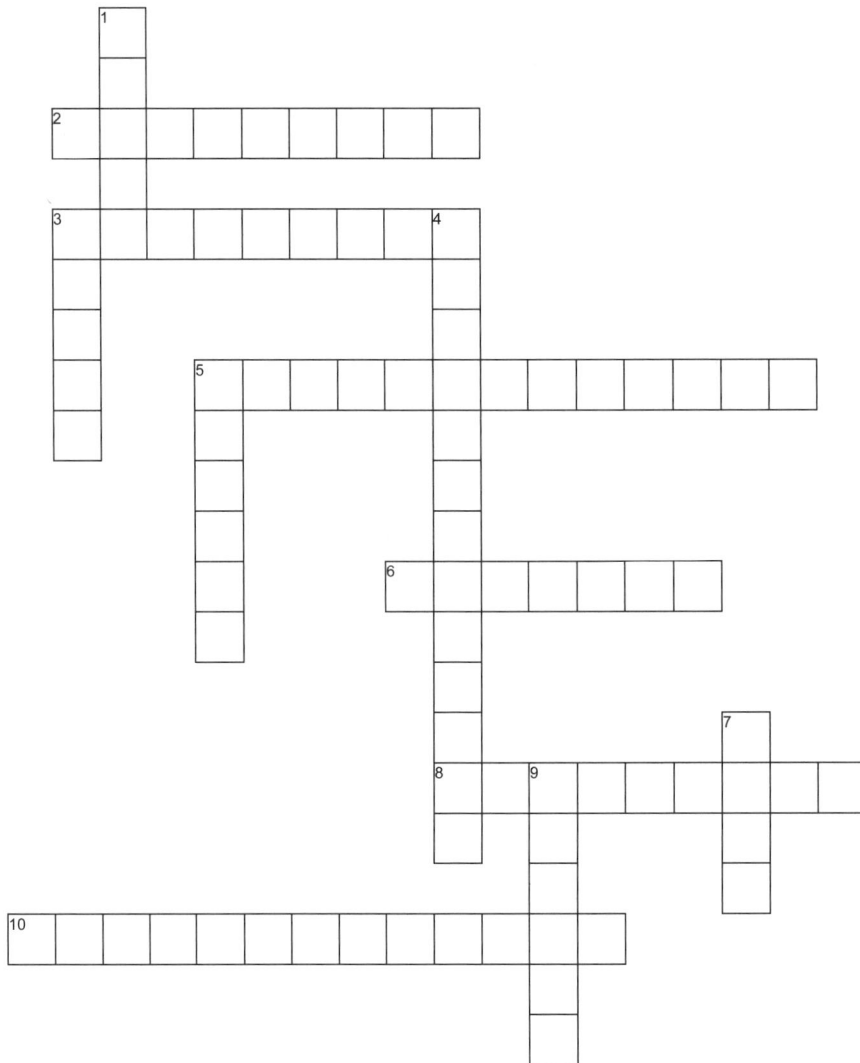

Across

2 What could happen if you have unprotected sex?

3 This food from the sea is bad for a pregnant lady to eat, especially when it's raw

5 This happens when the sperm meets the egg

6 This professional looks after the mother and unborn baby and usually assists with the birth

8 When an egg is released from the ovary this process is called…

10 The cord that links the baby with the mother (2 words)

Down

1 This usually happens after 9 months of being pregnant

3 Millions of these swim towards the egg

4 This professional supports the mother and baby for the first five years after the birth of the baby

5 Another word for the unborn baby

7 Fruit and vegetables make up part of a healthy…

9 Place in the body where the baby grows, sometimes called the womb

CFC6

AC 3.1

9.A9 Buying baby equipment

You are on a trolley dash. You have £400 to spend on items for a newborn baby. You need to buy the equipment for a new baby and their nursery.

Using catalogues list the items you will need on the shopping list below. Remember to keep within your budget. To do this you must include the prices for everything that you buy.

It is a good idea to start with a quick think on the whiteboard of what you need – for example, cot, pram, bedding, etc.

Shopping list	£ price
Total	£

CFC6
AC 3.1

9.A10 New parent responsibilities

Find these words in the grid below:

RESPONSIBILITY	BUDGET	FAMILY	SOCIALISING
PLAY	BONDING	NIGHT FEEDS	CUDDLES
ROUTINE	CLEANLINESS	SHELTER	SAFETY

R	E	S	P	O	N	S	I	B	I	L	I	T	Y	A
Q	W	E	O	N	D	I	N	U	M	U	M	R	A	B
N	E	O	N	I	P	D	A	D	A	P	L	A	L	I
B	O	N	D	I	N	G	M	G	N	O	P	I	P	L
O	B	E	I	L	K	Y	E	E	U	A	M	G	L	I
N	S	R	P	R	I	N	B	T	O	I	L	K	B	T
F	G	N	I	S	I	L	A	I	C	O	S	S	H	Y
E	P	X	O	T	A	L	L	Y	U	O	H	A	N	D
S	A	F	E	T	Y	O	L	O	D	P	E	K	D	E
K	L	S	A	F	O	I	Y	E	D	A	L	F	R	N
A	Z	O	M	C	M	P	B	E	L	A	T	R	A	I
H	A	P	P	A	R	N	E	D	E	N	E	I	G	T
A	I	M	F	A	M	V	I	O	S	A	R	J	P	U
N	I	G	H	T	F	E	E	D	S	O	F	L	O	O
M	Y	S	S	E	N	I	L	N	A	E	L	C	L	R

9.A11 Support for parents

What support can the people and organisations below offer to parents? Draw lines to match two boxes on the right to each of the boxes on the left.

Midwife	1. Helps parents back into work
	2. Offers preventative services such as immunisation
Health visitor	3. A national charity working for and with single parents
	4. Offers confidential advice on people's rights
Gingerbread	5. Will be at the delivery (birth) of the baby
	6. Supports the provision of childcare for under fives
Citizens Advice Bureau	7. Provides a helpline for single parents
	8. Carries out antenatal checks
Sure Start	9. Provides free information and advice on money problems
	10. Supports a child's development milestones

9.H1 Family support

Sure Start brings together childcare, early education, health and support services for families with children under 5 years old. It works with parents-to-be, parents, carers and children to encourage the physical, intellectual and social development of babies and young children so that they can flourish at home and when they get to school.

Sure Start Children's Centres offer:

- early learning and full day care provision for children (minimum ten hours a day, five days a week, 48 weeks a year)
- teachers to lead the development of learning at the centres
- health services for families, including antenatal services
- parental outreach
- family support services
- a base for a childminder network
- support for children and parents with special needs
- links to Jobcentre Plus
- support and outreach services to parents and carers, and children who have been identified in need of them
- information and advice to parents and carers
- support to childminders
- planned activities for children and carers and drop-in sessions at the centre.

Citizens Advice Bureau helps people resolve their legal, financial and other problems by providing free information and advice, and by influencing policy makers.

The Citizens Advice service aims to:

- provide the advice people need for the problems they face
- improve the policies and practices that affect people's lives.

The service provides free, independent, confidential and impartial advice to everyone on their rights and responsibilities. They deal with issues such as debt, benefits, housing, employment, consumer issues, relationships, family matters, health, education, discrimination, immigration and the law.

Gingerbread provides advice and practical support for single parents. They offer a helpline and a website packed full of useful information. Gingerbread work to improve the lives of all single parent families.

It's not just the practical aspects of life as a single parent that they can help with: separating from a partner or bringing up children alone often raises a mixture of practical and emotional issues. Their fact sheets look at situations ranging from what you need to think of when separating, to what your rights are during pregnancy. They also offer advice for parents under the age of 18.

Midwives do not have a nine-to-five job – they usually work on a rota to provide 24 hour care for the mum-to-be during pregnancy, throughout labour and during the period after a baby's birth. Midwives provide full antenatal care; classes, clinical examinations and screening. They also teach new mums how to feed and bathe their babies before handing over care to a health visitor.

Health visitors support families and young children in areas such as:

- immunisation
- healthy eating for infants, children and adults
- coping with minor illnesses
- behaviour problems, e.g. sleeping and routines
- a child's developmental milestones.

Introduction

This chapter covers:

L2 Unit CFC19 Self development

L1 Unit CFC16 Preparing for your next steps

This chapter is all about self development and getting ready for the next steps – whether another course or employment.

It is recommended that you cover Unit CFC19 first. The type of activities contained in this pack will help to bring it to life and enable learners to relate it to their own experience. Unit CFC19 is personal to the student, so the information will be personal to each particular learner. Unit CFC16 is more general and covers information about getting ready for employment which applies to everyone.

(NB These topics require sensitive handling. For some learners stretch beyond the level of this course may be difficult. Other courses of same level may be an option for some learners as a progression route.)

Learning outcomes

Unit CFC19

Unit CFC19 has five learning outcomes:

1. Recognise the significance of own achievements and interests to own development.
2. Recognise own strengths and areas for further development.
3. Understand how a person's learning style influences career and education choices.
4. Be able to set personal goals and objectives.
5. Be able to make action plans to achieve personal goals.

Teacher checklist

✓ What are learners' achievements and personal interests and how can these benefit them in reaching their goal of employment in childcare?

✓ Identify personal strengths and try to improve weaknesses

✓ Look at the importance of further development in the field of childcare and have a realistic understanding of what they need to do to reach their goal

✓ Matching own skills to the skills of professionals

✓ Understanding different ways of learning

✓ Personal goals and action plan to meet those goals

✓ Learners should – with guidance – be able to set up own goals and action the steps they need to achieve goals

---

Unit CFC16

Unit CFC16 has four learning outcomes:

1. Know about personal career goals.
2. Understand opportunities for training and work.
3. Know how to prepare for work or training.
4. Know about the recruitment process.

Teacher checklist

✓ Next steps in training and employment: entry requirements for training courses or jobs

✓ Available opportunities to progress in childcare

✓ How to prepare for work or training – understanding the different personal skills needed for different roles

✓ Preparing for interview: application forms, CVs, letter writing

✓ Practise interviews

✓ Personal presentation, hygiene, dress code, good manners, politeness

Additional guidance for delivery

Be very positive when you are approaching Unit CFC19 but remember to be honest too. Some learners may not be able to achieve all the goals they set for themselves – help them avoid setting themselves up for failure. Give learners plenty of support as they decide on their goals and the steps they must take to achieve them.

Most colleges encourage learners to complete a learning styles questionnaire. Learners could revisit these as a starting point when they are tackling Activity 10.A4.

When looking at the opportunities for progression in childcare, invite speakers into the classroom, e.g. a day nursery employee or a Connexions adviser. Provide information leaflets and sample job application forms. Stress the importance of well written letters and properly addressed envelopes – first impressions count. (Practising these things will also contribute to Functional skills literacy.) Putting together a professional CV is also an important part of getting ready for work.

Role play interviews if learners are confident enough – it will make the work on this section more immediate and realistic and is a great way of demonstrating dos and don'ts. (This activity also works very well if two tutors carry out the role play with learners invited to make comments.)

As a group, or on an individual basis, ask the learners to complete the interactive **Knowledge check** to finish the chapter.

Further resources

www.cache.org.uk

http://jobseekers.direct.gov.uk

https://nextstep.direct.gov.uk/Pages/Home.aspx

http://www.direct.gov.uk/en/EducationAndLearning/14To19/index.htm

http://career-advice.monster.co.uk/

http://yp.direct.gov.uk/14-19prospectus/

Answers to activities

10.A8

T	R	A	I	N	I	N	G	B	J	L	K
S	C	V	Y	T	E	T	H	K	I	C	P
A	Z	O	X	D	J	R	J	N	B	A	T
U	C	P	N	F	A	V	T	B	K	R	Q
R	M	Q	F	N	R	A	G	Y	N	E	F
E	W	C	V	W	E	B	S	I	T	E	S
S	Z	T	B	Y	H	X	E	T	Y	R	D
O	Q	U	T	B	B	V	I	R	D	S	S
U	W	T	U	B	S	S	F	O	B	T	E
R	E	O	R	C	H	S	H	A	N	F	H
S	C	R	C	G	R	B	H	S	A	S	N
E	G	Z	B	W	G	R	B	J	A	A	H
S	M	S	T	C	E	P	S	O	R	P	G
D	I	R	E	C	T	G	O	V	X	Q	Z

- prospects
- tutor
- resources
- training
- directgov
- connexions
- careers
- websites

10.A10

- Employee – someone who works for an employer
- Closing date – the date the application form must be sent back to the employers asking for an interview for the job
- Job description – a list of what the job entails – what you would have to do
- Employer – someone who pays for a job to be done
- Reference – from someone who knows you well and can support your job application saying what your strengths and weaknesses are
- Salary – the amount you will be paid in a year
- Application form – a form that is sent to you from employers which you need to fill in and send back before the closing date
- CV – a summary of your skills, personal details and qualifications which tell the employer about you

10.A11

- Good personal hygiene. Body odour, dirty hair, poor hand and nail care are very unprofessional. Bad breath – whether from smoking or not cleaning your teeth – is a 'no go' when going for interview.

- Dress code for interviews – don't go to an interview in the clothes, make-up and jewellery you would wear to a party.

- Research the job you have applied for – always try to find out more about the job. Check to see if the organisation is on the Internet – most schools and day nurseries have a web page.

- Prepare for the journey to the interview. Find out about bus times or parking spaces if you are getting a lift. Don't leave it to the day and time of interview – you could get lost.

- Be safe – always let someone, e.g. parents, know where the interview is if the area doesn't look safe – be very careful. For more information on how to keep safe, check www.suzylamplugh.org

- Arrive on time – always arrive on time for an interview. If you are going to be late, ring and let the person who is interviewing you know. Being late is not a good start.

- Make a good first impression – remember, first impressions mean a lot. Offer to shake hands with the people interviewing you. Think about how you sit during interview and keep your body language positive.

- Be polite and remember your manners – be polite and say goodbye and thank you at the end of the interview. You might meet these people again in the future if you are not successful this time.

Chapter 10 Personal development

Overview of resources

Resources	Teaching notes	Link to Student Book	Link to Units and assessment criteria
10.A1 Strengths and weaknesses	This activity can be done individually by the learners or as a class activity. Learners should write down two of their strengths and two weaknesses. If you are using this as a class activity the learners can write on 'post it' notes. Draw two columns onto the board and head them 'strengths' and 'weaknesses'. Learners can stick their words into the appropriate columns. Learners can look at the different qualities and discuss, e.g. can any of the weaknesses be strengths or vice versa? It is possible to extend this activity by suggesting other words and qualities such as: empathetic, sensitive, loud, patient, sympathetic, sporty, fit, motivated, etc. Ask the learners if they understand the word and whether it would be required when working in a childcare setting.	p.204–5	**CFC19** AC 2.1, 2.2
10.A2 Achievements and interests	Learners need to think about two personal goals that they have already achieved and what they had to do to get them, how long it took, how difficult it was, etc. They should be encouraged to identify ways in which each achievement and the skills and qualities learned could be transferred to other areas. It may be a good idea to give them an example on the board such as a first aid certificate.	p.202–3	**CFC19** AC 1.1
10.A3 Skills and qualities needed in childcare	Learners have already been thinking about their skills and qualities and they now need to extend these into their role as a childcare practitioner. Learners should complete the boxes on the left to show an understanding of each of the skills in the right-hand column. Some learners may be able to add to the list.	p.206	**CFC19** AC 2.1, 2.3
10.A4 Learning styles	Learners may have completed a learning styles questionnaire during their induction week and it would be useful to refer back to this during this session. Learners should be encouraged to think about how they learn. Working in pairs, learners list factors that affect their learning in the classroom. In the second column they should write changes they could make to the environment to enhance the learning taking place.	p.206–7	**CFC19** AC 3.1
10.A5 Personal goals	This activity helps learners to focus on their goals. Learners can use the star templates to write down their achievements and plot their own progress. This can be carried on throughout the course they are undertaking and placed with their Individual Learning Plans; it can also be used to set goals to be achieved in the future.	p.208–9	**CFC19** AC 4.1

Resources	Teaching notes	Link to Student Book	Link to Units and assessment criteria
10.A6 Action plan	This activity allows learners to think about the direction in which they are heading. It can be used to list short- and long-term goals, think about how they are going to achieve them and how long they should take. Learners need to be realistic and tutor guidance may be necessary.	p.210–11	**CFC19** AC 4.2, 5.1
10.A7 Steps to employment	Learners should list their personal qualifications and any job history, including paper rounds or babysitting. They need to think about the specific qualifications they will need to get the job they would like to do; this may require them to carry out a research task. Finally, they need to make an action plan to help them to achieve their aim; tutor guidance and course information will be required here and guest speakers could enhance the learning further.	p.214–15	**CFC16** AC 1.1, 1.2
10.A8 Barriers to achieving your goals	This activity highlights factors which may prevent learners from achieving their goals. It can be used to elicit discussion on how setbacks and problems can be resolved or minimised to prevent the learner being demotivated. The rain cloud can be drawn onto the board and problems suggested for debate by the class. Sensitive issues may arise and the tutor needs to be ready for this. Question 2 on the activity sheet is a wordsearch that suggests where learners may find help and support.	p.215	**CFC16** AC 1.3, 2.1
10. H1 Training and development opportunities	This handout gives advice on training opportunities available to learners; these will vary according to your centre and geographical location, so you could edit and adapt the handout to reflect what is available locally.	p.216	**CFC16** AC 2.2, 3.3
10. H2 Qualifications for employment	This handout looks at the childcare qualifications available to learners and asks learners to consider why functional skills are important in this area.	p.217	**CFC16** AC 2.3
10.A9 Personal skills wall	Learners are encouraged to 'build a skill wall'. This can be done on the sheet or learners can print off statements and build a wall from play bricks, which they can add to as skills are acquired. Future bricks can be inspired by the 'need to improve' table at the bottom of the sheet, which learners need to complete.	p.218–19	**CFC16** AC 3.1
10.A10 Steps to recruitment	This word and phrase matching activity can be done with flash cards or as a domino game. Learning can be extended by taking in physical items to illustrate the various things such as application forms, CVs and job descriptions. Discussion should also be encouraged to extend language, e.g. words such as salary, annual, pro rata, wages, etc.	p.224–25	**CFC16** AC 4.1

Resources	Teaching notes	Link to Student Book	Link to Units and assessment criteria
10.A11 Preparing for interview	For this activity learners need to think about interview techniques. Thought showers from small groups with class feedback will lead into the activity sheet. Once this activity has taken place, learners can practise role play activities such a making a call to say that they will be late, greeting interviewers, etc.	p.226–27	**CFC16** AC 4.2
Electronic resources			
10.PPT1 Self development	10.PPT1 introduces aspects of personal development, asking learners to identify their strengths and weaknesses and learning styles. Learners are encouraged to think about personal goals and what they might need to do to reach them.		
10.PPT2 Next steps	10.PPT2 invites learners to consider what they will do next – another course, an apprenticeship, seek work or look for a different career? Letters of application, CVs and interviews are introduced.		
Knowledge Check	Interactive quiz covering learning from the units in the chapter for consolidation purposes. You could run the quiz via the VLE with learners during the first session to see how much they already know; it could be done again later to see how much progress they have made. Alternatively, more independent learners could have a go at completing the quiz on their own.		

10.A1 Strengths and weaknesses

1. Write two of your strengths and two of your weaknesses into the boxes below.

Weakness	Weakness	Strength	Strength

Look at the qualities you have chosen. Can any of the weaknesses be turned into strengths? (For example, if 'emotional' is seen as a weakness, how can this be seen as a strength?)

2. Think about your role in working with children. What sort of qualities would be good or bad? Write as many strengths and weaknesses as you can. An example of each has been given for you.

Weakness	Strength
Shy	Caring

3. Discuss your answers with the group.

10.A2 Achievements and interests

Think of two achievements. They could be something you did at college or school or something you have done outside formal school education, for example something to do with sports or air cadets or the Guiding association. Then answer the following questions:

Achievement 1

1. What did you achieve?

2. How did you achieve this – what did you have to do?

3. How do you think the skills you have gained from this achievement have helped your development so far?

Achievement 2

1. What did you achieve?

2. How did you achieve this – what did you have to do?

3. How do you think the skills you have gained from this achievement have helped your development so far?

10.A3 Skills and qualities needed in childcare

This activity looks at your skills and qualities and compares them to the requirements needed to work in childcare.

Fill in the boxes in the left-hand column to match any skills and qualities you have with the skills needed by a childcare practitioner. If you can think of any more skills, add them to the bottom of the table.

Personal skills and qualities	Childcare practitioners skills
	Understanding what confidentiality means
	Being an active listener
	Understanding parents are the prime carers
	Being a good communicator
	Excellent attendance and time keeping
	Positive attitude to work
	Understanding that ongoing training is important
	Aware of personal hygiene and dress code

10.A4 Learning styles

We all learn in different ways.

- Some people learn by watching and copying.
- Some people learn by listening and then doing.
- Some people learn by reading and then doing.

1. Which is the best way that you learn? Think carefully before you write anything down.

2. What things affect your learning? It could be the room you are learning in – think about what you would like to change.

   Work in pairs to make a list of things that affect your learning. In the second column write what changes you would make. An example has been given to start you off.

Factors that affect learning	Changes you would like to make
Classroom too hot	*Open windows and turn radiators off*

10.A5 Personal goals

Complete the chart – the top star is your final goal in your top job, but you need to work your way towards it.

Start with the bottom star and write your achievements so far.

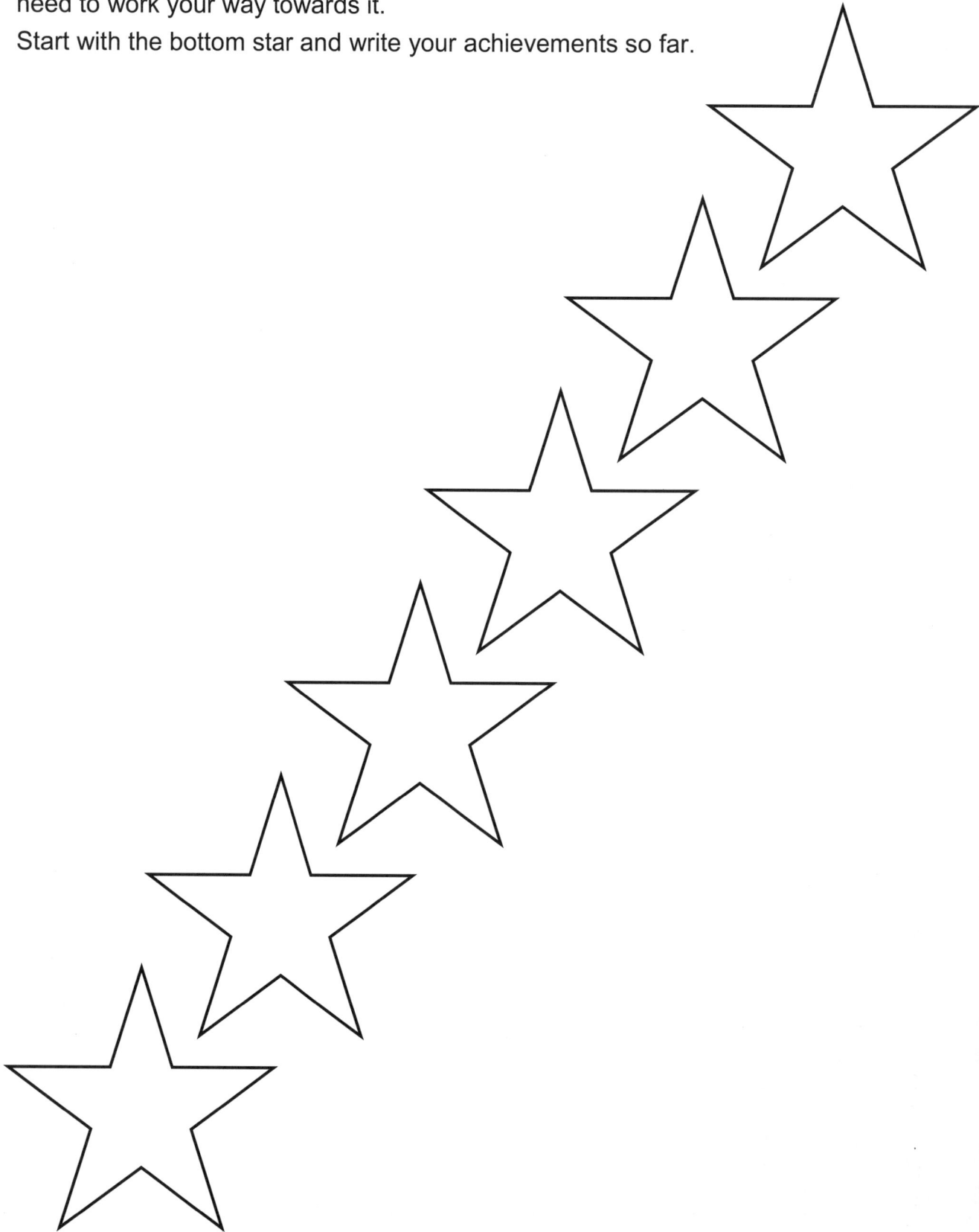

10.A6 Action plan

CFC19
A.C. 4.2, 5.1

1. Complete the action plan to show the goals and steps you need to take. Make sure your goals are SMART. Ask your tutor for guidance if you need it. An example of each has been given to you.

2. Use a ruler to underline each row after you have written it.

Personal goals	Actions I need to take to meet my goals	Time allowed	Review of how much I have achieved so far	When I expect to reach my goal
To complete L1 literacy	Attend all classes and do my best	6 months	Building my portfolio, finished two pieces of work with good marks	By the end of term 3 – June 2011

10.A7 Steps to employment

1. Think about what you have already achieved, for example coming to college is a huge achievement.

List the qualifications and skills you have gained so far – include things you have done outside school too, for example if have you had a job (a paper round, or babysitting jobs).

2. What qualifications do you need to do the job you would like to do?

Check with the information centre at your local training college to see if they have any leaflets on training for the job you would like to do. List the qualifications you need to get onto the courses you need to become qualified.

3. What steps do you have to do to get the job qualifications of your choice? What are the requirements of the courses?

Action plan:

CFC16
A.C. 1.3, 2.1

10.A8 Barriers to achieving your goals

1. List the things that may stop you from getting your dream job. Have a quick think and write your answers in the box below.

Things which might stop me getting my dream job…

2. Who or where might you go to for support in achieving your personal goals? See if you can find the hidden words. There are eight of them.

T	R	A	I	N	I	N	G	B	J	L	K
S	C	V	Y	T	E	T	H	K	I	C	P
A	Z	O	X	D	J	R	J	N	B	A	T
U	C	P	N	F	A	V	T	B	K	R	Q
R	M	Q	F	N	R	A	G	Y	N	E	F
E	W	C	V	W	E	B	S	I	T	E	S
S	Z	T	B	Y	H	X	E	T	Y	R	D
O	Q	U	T	B	B	V	I	R	D	S	S
U	W	T	U	B	S	S	F	O	B	T	E
R	E	O	R	C	H	S	H	A	N	F	H
S	C	R	C	G	R	B	H	S	A	S	N
E	G	Z	B	W	G	R	B	J	A	A	H
S	M	S	T	C	E	P	S	O	R	P	G
D	I	R	E	C	T	G	O	V	X	Q	Z

10.A9 Personal skills wall

1. Think about what skills you have. Maybe it's helping at home, looking after a pet or being a good neighbour. Think about how you behave in class: do you meet deadlines with your homework or support someone in class who is not as able as you are to do work? See how many bricks you can fill in on the skills wall.

I always take my dog for a walk twice a day		

	I always meet my assignment deadlines

2. Now think about other things you do that you may need to improve – fill in the table below.

List the skills you would like to improve (see example)	What do you need to do to improve these skills?
Attendance	*I need to attend all my classes 100%*

10.A10 Steps to recruitment

Do you know what each of the words below means? Cut out all the boxes and on a piece of card match up the right meanings to each word.

Employee	A form that is sent to you from employers which you need to fill in and send back before the closing date.
Closing date	The amount you will be paid in a year.
Job description	Someone who pays for a job to be done.
Employer	The date the application form must be sent back to the employers asking for an interview for the job.
Reference	A summary of your skills, personal details and qualifications which tell the employer about you.
Salary	Someone who works for an employer.
Application form	From someone who knows you well and can support your job application saying what your strengths and weaknesses are.
Curriculum Vitae (CV)	A list of what the job entails – what you would have to do.

10.A11 Preparing for interview

Draw lines to match the boxes on the left to the correct boxes on the right.

Good personal hygiene	Always arrive on time for an interview. If you're going to be late, ring and let the person interviewing you know. Being late is not a good start.
Dress code for interviews	Find out about bus times or parking spaces if you are getting a lift. Don't leave it to the day and time of interview – you could get lost.
Research the job you have applied for	Always let someone, e.g. parents, know where the interview is if the area doesn't look safe – be very careful. For more information on how to keep safe, check out the Suzy Lamplugh Trust website.
Prepare for the journey to the interview	Be polite and say goodbye and thank you at the end of the interview. You might meet these people again in the future if you are not successful this time.
Be safe	Don't go to an interview in the clothes, make-up and jewellery you would wear to a party.
Arrive on time	Always try to find out more about the job. Check to see if the organisation is on the Internet – most schools and day nurseries have a web page.
Make a good first impression	Body odour, dirty hair, poor hand and nail care are very unprofessional. Bad breath – whether from smoking or not cleaning your teeth – is a 'no go' when going for interview.
Be polite and remember your manners	Remember, first impressions mean a lot. Offer to shake hands with the people interviewing you. Think about how you sit during interview and keep your body language positive.

10.H1 Training and development opportunities

Sometimes if you want a certain kind of job, you have to undertake other courses that will give you qualifications to support your chosen career. If you want to work with children, not only do you have to get a suitable qualification at the right level, you would need to do a first aid course (a paediatric first aid course is good as it is just about working with children).

You may need to do a food hygiene course because you will be expected to provide suitable food or snacks. You need to learn about the storage of food to prevent food poisoning too if you are working in day care where children may stay from 8 a.m. to 6 p.m.

Creative activities can be another qualification you could add to your CV. These kinds of courses give you many ideas of what to do with the young children you will be working with.

Learning about other cultures and different religions is very important when working with children. Celebrating differences helps to make children feel like they belong. For example, Diwali is a Hindu festival of light. This should be celebrated as well as Christmas – a Christian festival. We are a multicultural society and should therefore know about other festivals and beliefs.

Find out what other short courses are available at your place of study. You may already be doing short courses alongside your main qualification. Remember to add these to your CV.

10.H2 Qualifications for employment

Getting the right qualifications and finding a job can be difficult. Choose college courses which are appropriate for what you want to do.

There are many childcare courses delivered by colleges and other training providers. These courses range from Entry Level to Level 3 and beyond.

You can also train on the job. There are childcare apprenticeships and work-based learning qualifications such as the Level 2 Certificate for the Children and Young People's Workforce.

Entry Level 3 and Level 1 courses in childcare do not qualify you for employment in childcare. Instead, they are seen as stepping stones to help you access higher level courses. These higher level courses will allow you to work towards getting a job in childcare.

You should also think about your achievements in literacy and maths. You may be working towards these in English and maths functional skills. These functional skills are really important in helping you to reach your dream job. Can you think why?

Think about what would happen if you sent an application letter full of spelling mistakes in it – do you think you would be offered a job?